NONPROFIT ESSENTIALS

The Development Plan

NONPROFIT ESSENTIALS

The Development Plan

Linda Lysakowski, ACFRE

John Wiley & Sons, Inc.

This book is printed on acid-free paper. ∞

Copyright © 2007 by John Wiley & Sons, Inc. All rights reserved.

Wiley Bicentennial Logo: Richard J. Pacifico

Published by John Wiley & Sons, Inc., Hoboken, New Jersey.

Published simultaneously in Canada.

For general information on our other products and services, or technical support, please contact our Customer Care Department within the United States at 800-762-2974, outside the United States at 317-572-3993 or fax 317-572-4002.

Wiley also publishes its books in a variety of electronic formats. Some content that appears in print may not be available in electronic books.

For more information about Wiley products, visit our web site at http://www.wiley.com.

Library of Congress Cataloging-in-Publication Data:

ISBN 978-0470-11797-2

Printed in the United States of America

10 9 8 7 6 5 4 3 2 1

The AFP Fund Development Series

The AFP Fund Development Series is intended to provide fund development professionals and volunteers, including board members (and others interested in the nonprofit sector), with top-quality publications that help advance philanthropy as voluntary action for the public good. Our goal is to provide practical, timely guidance and information on fundraising, charitable giving, and related subjects. The Association of Fundraising Professionals (AFP) and Wiley each bring to this innovative collaboration unique and important resources that result in a whole greater than the sum of its parts. For information on other books in the series, please visit:

http://www.afpnet.org

The Association of Fundraising Professionals

The Association of Fundraising Professionals (AFP) represents 28,000 members in more than 185 chapters throughout the United States, Canada, Mexico, and China, working to advance philanthropy through advocacy, research, education, and certification programs. The association fosters development and growth of fundraising professionals and promotes high ethical standards in the fundraising profession. For more information or to join the world's largest association of fundraising professionals, visit

www.afpnet.org.

2004–2007 AFP Publishing Advisory Committee

Linda L. Chew, CFRE
Associate Director, Alta Bates Summit Foundation

Nina P. Berkheiser, CFRE
Principal Consultant, Your Nonprofit Advisor

D. C. Dreger, ACFRE
Senior Campaign Director, Custom Development Systems (CDS)

Samuel N. Gough, CFRE, Chair
Principal, The AFRAM Group

Audrey P. Kintzi, ACFRE
Chief Advancement Officer, Girl Scout Council St. Croix Valley

Robert J. Mueller, CFRE
Vice President, Hospice Foundation of Louisville

Maria Elena Noriega
Director, Noriega Malo & Associates

Leslie E. Weir, MA, ACFRE
Director of Gift Planning, Health Sciences Centre Foundation

Sharon R. Will, CFRE
Director of Development, South Wind Hospice

John Wiley & Sons

Susan McDermott
Senior Editor (Professional/Trade Division), John Wiley & Sons

AFP Staff

Jan Alfieri
Manager, New Product Development

Walter Sczudlo
Executive Vice President & General Counsel

This book is dedicated to my children, grandchildren, and great-grandchildren, who provide daily inspiration to me: Patty, Tom, Ben, and Eli Downing; Vicki and Jim McIlwaine; Jason, Kathy, Nathan, and Kayleigh Foreman; Katie Foreman; Isabel Diaz; Joe Lysakowski; John, Maggie, Ariana, Stef, and Rachel Lysakowski; Matthew Lysakowski and Kate Spang.

Acknowledgments

I would like to thank the people with whom I have worked in my development career at Alvernia College and the Foundation for the Reading Public Museum, and the many associates and clients of Capital Venture who have helped me learn the importance of good planning. I especially want to thank the numerous friends and associates I have met through the international Association of Fundraising Professionals, Charity Channel, and the local chapters of AFP in which I have been involved.

In particular, I would like to thank those who contributed directly to this book: Kelly Aitland; Shirlene Courtis, CFRE; Stuart Golder; Margaret Guellich, CFRE; Sue Kreeger, CFRE; Rosemary Mahoney; Anne Peyton, CFRE; and Laura Scott.

About the Author

Linda Lysakowski (Las Vegas, NV) is the president/CEO of Capital Venture, a consulting and training firm specializing in capital and endowment campaigns and other fundraising services. She is one of only 78 people worldwide to hold the Advanced Certified Fundraising Executive designation. Named by both the Eastern Pennsylvania's and the Las Vegas, NV chapters of AFP "Outstanding Fundraising Executive of the Year" in 2001, and a magna cum laude graduate of Alvernia College, Linda is also a graduate of AFP's Faculty Training Academy and was the first recipient of AFP's Barbara Marion Award for outstanding leadership. She has been a speaker at local, regional, and national fundraising conferences for more than 10 years. She has authored two booklets in the AFP Ready Reference Series (*Establishing Your Development Office* and *Getting Ready for a Capital Campaign*) as well as articles for related newsletters and other nonprofit publications (*Charity Channel, CASE Currents, International Journal of Nonprofit and Voluntary Sector Marketing*) and her book *Recruiting and Training Fundraising Volunteers* was published in 2005. She is also a contributing author to *The Fundraising Study—It's Not About The Money*.

Contents

Introduction

I n my first job as a development officer, I realized how important it was to have a solid development plan and to ensure that everyone in the department was well aware of this plan. I was fortunate to have a great mentor, the late Ralph Wolfe of Martz and Lundy, who helped me put together an annual fund plan. As I grew into more responsible positions, I realized how important it was that the annual fund and other components of the development program, such as the capital campaign and planned giving, were woven together into a seamless development program. The public relations function is also an integral part of the development office, and again I was fortunate in my first development job to work with a team of excellent professionals who understood the importance of the two offices working hand in hand.

In my 15 years as a consultant, I have found that many smaller nonprofits, and a fair amount of larger ones, fail at their development efforts due to lack of planning. They tend to put all their eggs in one basket, placing too much effort into what should be one small aspect of their development program, usually grants or special events. As a banker, I learned the 80/20 rule early in my professional career, and I realized early in my consulting practice that this rule was morphing into the 90/10 rule or even the 95/5 rule. I found that many organizations were spending 80, 90, or 95 percent of their time working on activities that generated 20, 10, or even just 5 percent of their funds. A solid, well-thought-out development plan will allow the development office to focus its energies on the 5, 10, or 20 percent of their donors who will be responsible for 80, 90, or 95 percent of the organization's gifts.

Another observation I have made over the years is that board members and other fundraising volunteers need to have clear-cut goals and understand the basic psychology of philanthropy, as well as have a basic knowledge of fundraising techniques that have proven successful. In order to avoid the well-meaning board member or volunteer who may lead the organization astray by focusing on a single fundraising effort such as a major special event (or worse yet, a series of smaller special events) that can consume the time and energies of staff, board, and volunteers, a development plan can help the entire organization focus on an integrated approach to fundraising. The involvement of board members, non-development staff, and volunteers in the planning process will also ensure their buy-in to the plan.

Whether your organization has a small budget or is a multimillion-dollar operation, whether you have no development staff or a staff of 20, your organization will benefit from having a dynamic development plan that creates enthusiasm, fosters a sense of confidence in the organization, and helps track success. It is my hope that this book will help the novice development officer and the seasoned professional, the volunteers and the entire staff of the organization understand the development planning process and that, after reading this book, members of the development office will be able to develop a plan that is a vital part of the organization's success in fulfilling its mission.

CHAPTER 1

Why a Development Plan

"Wisdom consists not so much in knowing what to do in the ultimate
as in knowing what to do next."
Herbert Hoover

After reading this chapter, you will be able to:

- List the reasons a development plan is critical to a successful development program.
- Name the components of a development plan.
- Develop a plan to utilize various methods of fundraising that will be included in the plan.

Many readers will recall from their childhood the story of Alice in Wonderland. After Alice fell down the rabbit hole, she met the Cheshire cat, sitting in a tree, whom she asked in which direction she should start walking.

The Cheshire cat, grinning, asked, "Well, Alice, where do you want to go?"

"I don't know," was Alice's reply.

"Well, then it really doesn't matter in which direction you walk."

Unfortunately, many development officers find themselves hurtling down that rabbit hole on a daily basis and, when lost in the woods, are not sure which way to go. Too bad they don't have that Cheshire cat offering his sage advice!

To exacerbate the problem, many development people, instead of having the time to carefully plan their development program, have been thrown into a situation where the organization has had no plan in the past from which to work and where the organization's leadership expects the development officer to work miracles. Why does this happen? Often, the development officer is the "new kid on the block," having been hired after the organization has already enmeshed itself in a lot of misguided information about the way fundraising should be done and may have had a number of false starts in the development arena. In the life cycle of a nonprofit organization, development often enters the scene at the maturity stage.

Carter McNamara, in his article "Basic Overview of Organizational Lifestyles," provides a chart developed by Richard L. Daft for his book *Organizational Theory and Design*, which lists the various components of a typical organization's life cycle.

	Birth	**Youth**	**Midlife**	**Maturity**
Size	Small	Medium	Large	Very large
Bureaucratic	Nonbureaucratic	Prebureaucratic	Bureaucratic	Very bureaucratic
Division of Labor	Overlapping tasks	Some departments	Many departments	Extensive, with small jobs and many job descriptions
Centralization	One-person rule	Two leaders rule	Two department heads	Top-heavy management
Formalization	No written rules	Few rules	Policy and procedure manuals	Extensive rules
Administrative Intensity	Secretary, no professional staff	Increasing clerical and maintenance	Increasing professional and staff support	Large—multiple departments

	Birth	Youth	Midlife	Maturity
Internal Systems	Nonexistent	Crude budget and information systems	Control systems in place—budget, performance, reports, etc.	Extensive—planning, financial, and personnel added
Lateral Teams, Task Forces for Coordination	None	Top leaders only	Some use of integrators and task forces	Frequent at lower levels to break down bureaucracy

McNamara cites another perspective on the life cycles of organizations from Judith Sharken Simon in *The Five Life Stages of Nonprofit Organizations*. While both of these approaches are helpful in understanding the life cycles of a nonprofit organization and how development fits into this life cycle, Simon's view may have more appeal to the typical nonprofit leader because it is less about structure and more about vision. She lists five stages:

- Stage One: Imagine and Inspire ("Can the dream be realized?")

- Stage Two: Found and Frame ("How are we going to pull this off?")

- Stage Three: Ground and Grow ("How can we build this to be viable?")

- Stage Four: Produce and Sustain ("How can the momentum be sustained?")

- Stage Five: Review and Renew ("What do we need to redesign?")

In looking at the typical life cycles of a nonprofit, they are similar to the life cycles of all living things. First, there is the embryonic stage, then infancy, followed by childhood, puberty, young adulthood, maturity, and finally old age. A nonprofit organization's life cycles are similar. The organization usually starts with a seed of an idea as some person or group of people come together with a vision to solve a perceived problem (Simon's Stage One). For example, a mother loses a child in a drunken driving accident, and MADD is born; a church group sees the need to feed the hungry and homeless, and a food kitchen is opened; a group of parents want better educational opportunities for their gifted children, and a private school is established; a community seeks to improve its cultural life, and a theater group evolves from this vision. As these organizations are birthed into infancy, their focus is on programs—who will provide the education, the food for the hungry, the advocacy, or the performances?

As these organizations move into childhood and adolescence, they see the need to become more organized. At that point, an executive director is usually hired to manage the organization and perhaps a financial officer to help complete the necessary reports and handle payroll as the staff begins to grow (Daft's Youth Stage). Usually, in young adulthood the organization sees a need to expand and perhaps increase community awareness in order to secure more support for their programs. Usually, at this period more program staff persons are brought on board, and a public relations or marketing person is often hired.

As the organization grows into maturity, it may find that the current mode of operation is not enough to sustain the organization or to allow it to grow. Government or foundation funding may have decreased or been cut altogether, special events may face increasing competition from other community events, and the founders have probably exhausted their initial funding. This is Simon's Stage Four—how can momentum be sustained?

In most cases, the development person is hired after the organization has already enmeshed itself in some basic fundraising programs; usually grant proposal writing and special events because these are development activities that most organizations can manage without designated development staff. Often, the executive director has come from a program background and is not strong in the areas of business or fund development, but as a program person has been involved in grant proposal writing. Likewise, many of the board members of a young organization have agreed to serve on the board because they have a passion for the work of the organization, but may not been carefully selected based on their various skills and talents, or connections that they have in the community. These board members have most likely been involved in special events at other organizations and have lots of ideas for fundraising events at this organization.

As the organization matures, it realizes that it needs some expertise in the areas of fundraising; however, its view of fund development may focus strictly on things that are familiar to it. Many program people have been involved with writing grant proposals for their individual programs, so executive directors who are program people will probably have the expertise to continue writing the proposals once they are in the executive director position. And almost all board members have been involved in one way or another with special events, so this area is within their comfort zone and they will focus all their energies on these fundraising events until they either get burned out or realize that development has a far-reaching scope beyond events.

What happens next is often that a development officer is hired and expected to work miracles. "How soon will the development officer be able to raise his or her salary and show a profit?" is a question often asked by boards and chief executive officers (CEOs). The answer is, "It depends." The difference between an organization that can quickly show results and one that will take more patience depends on the organization's understanding and availability of the prerequisites to a successful development program. What are some of the things can determine the success of a development program and how does the development plan assure success?

At the end of this chapter, there is a Philanthropic Profile Assessment Tool (Exhibit 1.1) to help assess the organization's level of commitment to fundraising and philanthropy. This is a helpful tool to use with board and executive management to help them understand the importance of their commitment to development if the development office is to succeed.

Where in these life cycles does the development plan fit? If an organization's leader is insightful, she or he will have at least a simple development plan from the very beginning. Often, the development plan comes into play during midlife or whenever the development officer is hired, but for many well-established organizations, the development plan is way of looking at a mature program (Stage Five for Simon, Maturity for Daft) and asking, "What do we need to redesign in our development operations?"

TIPS & TECHNIQUES

Some key elements of a successful development program are:

- The level of commitment of the board to assist with fundraising.

- The level of technology that is in place and/or the budget amount designated for technology needs of the development office.

- The organization's commitment to the professional development of its fundraising staff.

- The ability of the organization to create community awareness and build relationships.

- The diversity of funding streams and the variety of fundraising techniques used.

The development plan is an important tool to help development officers, whether they are new to the profession or senior-level professionals, implement and manage a well-integrated development program. Without a plan, like Alice, newer development officers will be lost in the woods. They will be pulled in many directions by the board, volunteers, and the executive director. They will spend most of their time trying to deal with the various events that the organization has been running, usually without any assessment of the viability of these events or the lost opportunity costs resulting from the excessive amount of time spent on event planning and implementation. They will take the shotgun approach to grant proposal writing, sending out proposals to as many potential funders as they can find, without taking the time to plan their approach to carefully researched funders, matching the funder's interest to the needs of the organization. Major donor identification, research, and solicitation will be done sporadically, if at all.

Even seasoned professionals can get caught up in the whims of board members and volunteers or the demands of their CEO if they don't have a carefully thought out development plan. Without a plan that contains measurable goals,

IN THE REAL WORLD

One development director reports that she is the third development person her organization has had in place during the past three years and that one of the projects that had always gone by the wayside was the planning process. She reports that it took her a good three months just to "learn the ropes" in a new organization. In addition to this hurdle, the organization had always hired inexperienced development people because they could not afford the salary that a more experienced development person would require. These "newbies" to fundraising generally did not have the expertise to develop a plan and spent most of their brief tenure at the organization trying to learn the profession of fundraising. At the same time, the board set unrealistic expectations for the development office, so the development staff found themselves scrambling to bring in the quick donations and had neither the time nor the expertise to develop lasting relationships with donors. This development officer wisely chose to work with the board on developing a realistic plan with reasonable goals.

In contrast, another development officer, well seasoned in the profession and working for larger institution with a strong fundraising history, has been successful in developing a detailed departmental operational plan that feeds into the institution's broader 10-year business plan. This plan includes specific tasks, deadlines, persons responsible, and priority status of each task. A detailed calendar is part of this organization's development plan. Because this institution has a larger development staff of experienced professionals, there was little board involvement in the plan itself, other than to approve it and understand their role in the implementation of the plan. This organization was also able to develop its plan without the use of outside consultants to guide the process.

it is hard to assess success, and harder still to justify the development budget, including staff salaries or increased staff positions. Often, especially in smaller organizations with newer development programs, board members and even staff can get caught up in "special event fever." Many times, a well-meaning volunteer or board member will come into a meeting saying, "Let's run a golf tournament; the XYZ organization just ran one and made $100,000." But has this enthusiastic volunteer taken into account that perhaps *this* organization has never run a golf tournament, knows nothing about golf, its board members do not play golf nor can they line up hole sponsors, and so on?

Another drawback of not having an integrated plan is that the organization may be losing money because it is not approaching its donors in the best way possible. For major donors, it will be necessary to make personal individual calls, and if the development officer is busy putting out fires and managing ongoing events and grants, he or she will not have time to plan a logical moves management system for major donors. *Moves management* is a process by which the organization identifies, cultivates, and solicits major donors according to a well-laid-out plan that is individualized for each prospective donor. This process is guided by the LAI principle, a theory based on the three elements of a successful major gift—linkage, ability, and interest. In order to receive a major gift from any donor, there must first be a careful analysis of the prospect's ability to give. Research must, therefore, be part of the development plan. Finding the right linkage—who is the best person to make the ask—is a key element of the major-gift process, and the development plan should lay out a process to identify this linkage through board members, staff, or other volunteers. Interest is the final element of the three requisites of a major gift (and all three must be present in order to receive a major gift), so the plan should include methods to identify and cultivate the prospective donor's interest in the programs of the organization. Even midrange donors have specific ways they want to be approached. For example, some will respond better to direct mail, others to telephone fundraising. Without a plan that includes a variety of approaches, a lot of money is often left on the table.

One of the most important reasons to have a development plan is so that the organization can assess its performance and make adjustments to fundraising programs where necessary. The plan must have a system to benchmark success and make adjustments to the strategies developed in the plan. The plan should be evaluated on a regular basis and progress reported to the board and management staff. This topic will be covered in more depth in Chapter 7.

TIPS & TECHNIQUES

Some of the principal successes organizations have reported as a result of having a development plan include:

- Increases marketing and visibility of the organization.

- Help the organization make business contacts.

- Makes it possible to track success of capital campaign.

- Points out areas on which the organization needs to focus.

- Helps keep the staff focused.

- Assists with writing the case for support and grant proposals.

- Assists the organization in gathering and sharing information with board and volunteers.

The Basic Elements of a Development Plan

The development plan should include goals and objectives for each of its components, as well as strategies and actions steps to achieve objectives. These should include a timeline, budget, and area of responsibility. One of the biggest mistakes many organizations make is to not carry the planning process far enough. Often, organizations spend a great deal of time, money, and energy developing goals, objectives, and strategies, but do not ask themselves three important questions about the action steps needed to support these goals, objectives, and strategies:

1. When is it going to be done?

2. Who is going to do it?

3. How much is it going to cost?

A good development plan will focus on all areas relating to the organization's fundraising program. These areas should include:

- Communication strategies and techniques.

- Donor relations, including stewardship and cultivation.

- Research strategies and techniques.

- Fundraising programs such as events, grants, direct mail, telephone fundraising, and personal solicitation.

- All constituencies, including individuals, corporations and businesses, foundations, and organizations.

- Technology and infrastructure.

- Human resources, including staff, board, and volunteers.

Andy Stanley tells us that visions often die because of inactivity. "It is discouraging to continue dreaming about something that appears to have no potential of ever happening. Besides, there is so much in life that must be done, why waste time dreaming about the impossible," Stanley says. This happens in many nonprofit organizations. The vision is there, but the resources and energy to make it happen may not be. The lack of a vision is usually not the problem for nonprofits—after all, wasn't the organization birthed from the vision of an individual or a group of people? Very seldom does one see a nonprofit organization that has no vision. Just talk with the staff and boards of any nonprofit, and only rarely will one come across an organization that is muddling along just because they have "always" existed and think they must continue to exist. Occasionally, one will find an organization like this, but in most cases, the organization's leaders can and do speak passionately about their vision to anyone who will listen.

More common, however, is the organization that has the vision but is just not sure how to make it happen. The organization itself must have a sound strategic plan, outlining the direction for its programs, its facilities, and its financial resources. The development plan is a crucial part of this strategic plan since it will enable the organization to fulfill its vision.

In his book, *Fund Raising*, James Greenfield says that strategic planning is important for the nonprofit organizations not just to measure its outcomes, but to study the results of its efforts and be able to deal with contingencies that may arise. He cites Lowell, Pearson, and Raybin's *Strategic Planning for Fundraising*, listing the reasons organizations undertake strategic planning for fundraising as:

- The strategic plan requires that the resources to fund the plan must be available.

- The organization may have a need for increased funding because of new or expanded programs.

- The organization has lost a major source of funding and needs to develop new strategies.

- The organization recognizes the need to not be dependent on a limited amount of funding sources.

- A new CEO or chief development officer (CDO) is on board.

- Enlarged board membership with more interest in fundraising activities.

- Demographic or economic shifts in the community.

- It has been more than four years since the organization evaluated its fundraising program.

The development plan must be a part of an organization's overall strategic or long-range plan if the organization is to be successful in reaching its goals. Financial resources must be found to fund any organization's growth, or even to maintain its status quo. The development plan will outline the methods to be used, the timelines in which to accomplish financial goals, and the budget for both human and financial resources needed by the development department. Sometimes, there is a crisis in funding streams—a government grant or contract is no longer available, a major event has failed, a major donor has pulled their funding. In cases like this, an integrated development plan becomes vital to the organization's future success, and sometimes to its very existence. A sound development plan covering a variety of funding streams will prevent this catastrophe from happening in the first place. But, if there was no plan in place, the development plan devised under a crisis situation will most likely be done quickly and with emphasis on immediate needs. This type of plan should be reevaluated under more stable circumstances, perhaps at the end of a year or six months when the crisis has been averted, to assure that it focuses on long-term stability.

Any change in the organization's human resources—a new CEO or development officer, a shift in attitudes about fundraising brought on by new board members—may lead to the need for a new or revised development plan, taking into account the additional resources available for development efforts. An organization seeking to expand its development program will often seek new board members who are skilled in major-gift fundraising and more willing to assume a fundraising role. This new resource for the development office should be taken into account when the plan is developed or revised. A new CEO who asks to see the development plan shows an interest in development and will most likely request a development plan quickly if there is not a plan in place already. Or they may want to place their own stamp of approval and/or insert their own personal interests and skills into the plan. New board or staff people who show an interest in development should be invited to help the CDO with the development plan. If an organization has not looked at its planning process for several years, it will require a fresh look at the community and the organization itself. Many factors may have changed within the community and the organization itself, opening up a whole new set of opportunities and threats to the development plan, for example, changing demographics in the community, economic conditions, new sources of funding, or the departure of current funding sources—all of which can have a drastic effect on the development plan. In addition, there may be new circumstances within the organization itself—new programs, a need for new facilities, additional staffing or loss of staff, many things that can affect the development plan. For this reason, it is important that a plan be revisited each year.

Summary

Organizations go through various life cycles, and development planning is essential to each of these cycles; however, most organizations do not get serious about fund development until they are reaching maturity. Organizations in their infancy may have a simpler plan but should, nonetheless, plan their fundraising activities from the beginning of the organization's life cycle. Those who do will be more successful at avoiding some common traps in the fundraising area, including:

- Not involving the board in fundraising.
- Becoming too dependent on one source of funding.
- Not investing in development staff.

A more mature organization should have a more detailed and complex development plan and should evaluate the strengths and weaknesses of its past development performance before beginning to plan for the future.

Some key elements of a successful development plan include:

- Board and staff involvement in the planning process.
- Willingness to invest in the professional development of development staff.
- Investing time and money into creating awareness of the organization in the community.
- Understanding the value of having diverse funding streams.

Many organizations get trapped in "event fever" or in grant proposal writing because these are usually the areas with which the staff and board are more familiar. It is important to consider a full range of development activities when preparing the development plan. It is also critical to ensure that there are bench-marks for success.

The plan should include overarching goals, broad strategies on how to reach these goals, more specific objectives, and detailed action steps on how to achieve each objective. The action steps must include budgets, timelines, and areas of responsibility.

Further Reading

McNamara, Carter. "Basic Overview of Organizational Life Cycles," www.managementhelp.org/org_thry/org_cycl.htm.

Daft, Richard L. *Organizational Theory and Design,* 6th ed. (Cincinnati, Oh.: South-Western Educational Publishing, 1997).

Simon, Judith Sharken. *The Five Life Stages of Nonprofit Organizations: Where You Are, Where You're Going, and What to Expect When You Get There.* (St. Paul, Minn.: Amherst H. Wilder Foundation, 2001).

Stanley, Andy. *Visioneering: God's Blueprint for Developing and Maintaining Personal Vision.* (Sisters, Ore.: Multnomah Publishers, 2005).

Greenfield, James M. *Fund Raising,* 2nd ed. (New York: John Wiley & Sons, 1999).

Greenfield, James M. *Strategic Planning for Fundraising* (New York: John Wiley & Sons, 1999), p. 46.

Philanthropic Profile Assessment Tool

1. Does the organization have a development office?

2. Do experienced professionals staff the development office?

3. Does the development budget include money for professional development (membership in professional organizations, conferences and workshops, books and periodicals, etc.) for the development staff?

4. Has the organization allocated a budget for a donor software system to manage fundraising activities?

5. Do the organization's staff members understand the importance of the development function? Do staff members support the development office's efforts?

6. Does the organization seek to hire development professionals that are certified (CFRE or ACFRE, FAHP, etc.) or assist current staff in obtaining credentials?

7. Does the chief development officer attend board meetings?

8. Is the board committed to development (do they give and get money for the organization)?

9. Is there a development committee on the board?

10. Does a development officer staff this committee?

11. Is there clerical support for the chief development officer?

12. Does the development staff act and look professional?

13. Is the development office in a prominent location, and does it have a professional appearance?

14. Does the organization support the Donor Bill of Rights?

15. Is the organization aware of and supportive of the AFP Code of Ethical Standards?

continued on the next page

16. Does the organization understand the importance of donor-centered fundraising?

17. Does the organization understand that it takes time to establish a development program, and that building relationships with donors is the key role of the development office?

18. Is the organization committed to working with consultants when it is appropriate to do so, and not expecting staff to manage major efforts such as a capital campaign?

19. Is the CEO involved in fundraising?

20. Are there volunteers involved in fundraising?

Give your organization 5 points for each "Yes" answer!

CHAPTER 2

Who Needs to Be Involved in the Planning Process?

"Who is wise? He [or she] who learns from everyone."
Benjamin Franklin

 ## After reading this chapter, you will be able to:

- List the various people who will be involved in the plan.
- Develop methods to include non–development staff in the planning process.
- Formulate a plan to involve volunteers, including board members, in the planning process.

In their book on organizational strategic planning, Michael Allison and Jude Kaye provide a chart listing who should be involved in the planning process, depending on the level of complexity of the plan. They list in a table the following people who are typically involved in organizational planning:

Level of Planning	Time Available	Personnel Involved	Depth of Analysis to Be Done
Abbreviated	One or two days	Smaller organizations—usually entire board and staff Larger organizations—entire board and staff representatives	Little or none

continued on the next page

Level of Planning	Time Available	Personnel Involved	Depth of Analysis to Be Done
Moderate	One to three months	Smaller organizations—usually entire board and staff Larger organizations—entire board and staff representatives Some external stakeholders provide input (clients and funders)	Some
Extensive	Six months or more	Large number, including extensive input from all major internal and external stakeholder groups	A lot: at a minimum includes data from stakeholders and objective data about operating environment

This chart is easily adaptable for development planning. The main difference for the people involved in development planning is that there is less board involvement and more staff involvement in the planning process, and generally development plans do not require input from external sources other than the volunteers who serve on the development committee.

The Development Staff

The chief development officer (CDO) should be the leader of the team that works on the development plan. While there are other people who need to be involved, it will be principally the work of the CDO to implement the plan. This CDO may have any one of a number of titles: vice president of institutional advancement, director of development, vice president for philanthropy, chief development officer, or any number of similar titles. However, every organization should have one person who is responsible for fundraising, and that is the person who will develop the plan. If there is no staff person on board, this role may fall to a board member, a volunteer, or a non–development staff person.

Where there is a full development department, the entire development staff should be involved in the process, as they will all be involved in making the plan

One development officer, newly promoted to become acting vice president after the vice president resigned, decided to include the staff members in the development planning process. She held weekly meetings with the staff, not only to have everyone update her on progress in their particular area, as her predecessor had done, but to provide an educational program for the entire development staff, including the receptionist, the data entry person, and the public relations department. Each staff meeting included an educational segment on various aspects of fundraising—telephone appeals, direct mail, major gifts, planned gifts, events, and so on. Once staff members got to see the whole picture, they became more aware of how their piece of the program affected the entire development process. When it came time for the plan to be updated, each person was invited to give input into the plan, including setting realistic timelines, identifying resources that were needed, and deciding which individual or team would be responsible for implementing each step of the plan. Productivity increased as a result of this inclusion of staff members who, prior to this time, had little input or understanding of the broad areas covered by the development department.

a workable tool to enhance and improve development office functions and results. Often, the support staff is under-utilized in the planning process. All development staff should be part of this important step. A staff member who knows what the plan involves and why each step in the plan is important to the outcome of the development program will be far more productive than one who only knows his or her little piece of the puzzle.

Non–Development Staff

It is also wise to bring in other staff members from the organization, who are outside the development office. Most organizations do not tap into the useful

TIPS & TECHNIQUES

Who is involved in the development planning process tends to be different depending on the size of the organization and the scope of the plan. Development officers surveyed reported the following people involved in their planning process:

Smaller Organizations	Larger Organizations
Director of development	CDO and other development staff
Consultant	Consultant
Board (no development staff)	Development staff with board approval

information held by program people and others within their organization, which can be extremely beneficial to the development office. Often, program people have valuable insights into helping develop the case for support as well as being the primary contact between the organization and its constituents. Teachers, nurses, maintenance staff, security guards, receptionists—all of these people come into contact with donors on a regular basis. The better these people understand the role of development within the organization, the more helpful they will be in presenting a good public image, identifying potential volunteers, and building relationships with prospective donors.

The development office, of course, plays the key role in the development plan. This should be one of the first things that a new development officer does upon accepting a position, and an annual plan should be done at the end of each fiscal year, to be implemented during the coming year. The CDO should first evaluate the past year's results and then list the goals for the coming year. Once she or he has a basic understanding of the areas on which the plan should focus, the rest of the development staff (assuming there is more than one person) should be brought in to help establish clear goals and objectives for the development program. If the development office is a one-person shop,

IN THE REAL WORLD

One development officer, new to her position, learned on the first day in the office, how critical it can be to involve non–development staff in the development program. She was just setting up her desk in her tiny office when a smiling face appeared at her door. It was an elderly teacher in the school for the arts at which this development officer had just accepted the position of its first director of development. The teacher said, "Sorry to interrupt you, but I understand you are here to help us raise money."

"That's correct," replied the new development director.

"Well, I know someone from whom I think we can get some money and I've been telling them for years they should approach this foundation, but no one ever listened to me."

"Let's go have lunch," said the new development officer, noticing that the clock said 11:30, "and you can tell me all about this foundation."

It turned out that the teacher had a former student who was now a program officer at a large foundation in a neighboring state. During lunch, the development officer asked the teacher to call her former student to see if she would accept a proposal; the development officer then drafted a formal proposal; and, after receiving the proposal, the program officer suggested she make a site visit to the school. The well-planned tour and, of course, a visit with her former teacher resulted in the largest gift this school had ever received.

Lesson learned: Listen to everyone in your organization—program people, clerical support, maintenance people, and so on, and involve them in the development planning process whenever it seems appropriate to do so.

he or she might at this time include other staff in the goal-setting process, such as the executive director, as well as key volunteers, in particular the development committee.

If there is no existing development program in the organization, some development officers will see this as a blessing, whereas others may view it as

TIPS & TECHNIQUES

One way to solicit input from staff members is to hold a focus group with non–development staff. Offer staff a free lunch on a workday in exchange for their ideas. Prepare a brief presentation (10 minutes), perhaps using a PowerPoint slide show summarizing the case for support and outlining the needs of the organization for funding.

Then briefly outline the development office's plan for raising the money to meet these needs and ask for their suggestions and ideas for prospective donors, development activities, and volunteer resources to help with fundraising. You can even make a game out of the planning process, awarding some token prizes for the staff members who come up with the most creative ideas for the development plan, identify potential donors, or recruit fundraising volunteers.

a curse. The good news is that there is nothing by which to compare their performance; the bad news is there is nothing by which to compare their performance! Without a track record of development, one of the big challenges of developing a workable plan is that it is difficult to set goals and benchmarks for tracking these goals. One cannot set a goal to increase alumni participation, for instance, if the organization has never approached its alumni for donations. However, overanalysis of past performance and dependence on methods used previously sometimes leads to the inability to be creative in developing new ideas for fundraising activities. Of course, without past records to analyze, the planning process will require much less time. It is important to realize that some development officers are better at creating a program from scratch, while others are good at analyzing past performance and building on it to improve the development department's performance. Recognizing this dichotomy, both the organization and the development officer should be able to find an appropriate match for the organization and themselves when hiring or being hired as new development staff. The organization's leadership should understand and feel comfortable with the work style of the CDO in developing and implementing the plan.

Even if there is no empirical data to analyze in the development office, there are some good baseline questions a new development officer can ask to assess the organization's readiness for fundraising. The development officer should start by looking at a few key areas:

- The board's willingness to become involved in fundraising.

- The level of support from the CEO.

- The infrastructure already in place.

- The opportunities for professional development.

- Any past donations the organization has received, even if unsolicited.

- The "natural prospects" the organization might have such as alumni, clients, volunteers, vendors, and so on.

The Philanthropic Profile Assessment Tool (Exhibit 1.1) found at the end of Chapter 1 will serve as a good resource to analyze the organization's potential for fundraising.

The CEO

The role of the executive director or CEO of the organization is also critical in the planning process. In particular, he or she should be aware of his or her role in implementing the plan. For example, how much of his or her time will be spent in cultivation and solicitation activities? At what events will his or her presence be required, and when are these events planned? Another, perhaps even more important, reason for involving the CEO in the planning process is so he or she is well aware of what resources will be needed by the development office in order to implement the plan. Sometimes the

One development officer found herself in a situation of starting a development program for a public museum when she was hired as their first development officer. Because the museum was publicly held and operated, they had never found a need to raise funds. In her first week on the job, she did a quick evaluation of the resources that were available and found:

- The board was small (eight people) but committed to enhancing their reach into the community by recruiting a larger board.

- The staff of the museum, while somewhat reluctant to embrace fundraising, had a great deal of information about donors to the museum's collection and the museum's history, and therefore were able to provide valuable information for the case for support.

- There was an active "Friends" group and a large pool of volunteer docents who could be helpful in fundraising.

- There was a donor database in place with the names of city employees who could be approached for financial support.

- There had been a successful event held several years prior, which could be resurrected.

- The museum director had written numerous successful government grants and would continue to handle this process.

- There was interest in the community in preserving the museum and assuring its future.

Within the first year, using these minimal tools, the development office was able to raise almost $400,000 by preparing an integrated development program that included resurrecting the special event, identifying new potential individual donors, further involving past donors in the museum's activities, implementing a corporate appeal, and, most importantly, growing the board from a group of 8 passionate people to 33 community leaders.

development office completes its plans in a vacuum and then wonders why the rest of the organization, and particularly their boss, do not buy into the plan. If the CEO agrees to the goals and objectives up front, the development office can then develop strategies with assurance that they will be supported by management.

In some cases, where there is no development officer, it will be the CEO who develops the plan. He or she, in many cases, serves as the CDO for the organization. If this is the case, the CEO may want to assign someone, an assistant or perhaps a board member, to take charge of the planning process details and lead the meetings.

It will also be important to include other non–development staff in the planning process. The CFO, for example, if not included in the planning process, can be an obstructive force in implementing the plan if he or she feels the resources are not available to fund new development initiatives or expand existing ones. The CFO, like the CEO, should be aware of the resources that will be need. The CFO also will want to know the timing of development activities so he or she can budget income and expenses accordingly.

It will also be helpful to include other staff members within the organization. For instance, it would helpful for the CDO to meet with the heads of all program-related departments to find out what their needs are for the upcoming year. These needs will be important to include in the case for support. And knowing that they had some input into the plan will increase the likelihood that key program staff people will be supportive of the development efforts. Program people should be somewhat involved in the process of determining what programs have a priority for funding, as this will help the development office prepare the case for support and special project fundraising activities. Of course, the reality is that every program person will think his or her area has top priority on the list of program needs, but involving the CEO and other key administrators can help establish realistic priorities for funding.

IN THE REAL WORLD

One organization attributes its success in implementing its development plan to the fact that it is part of an overall business plan developed by senior management. While the president did not take an active role in developing the resource development plan, he did stress its inclusion as part of the institution's overall plan and supported the efforts of the development office to develop realistic timelines and budgets, as well as allowing the development office to establish its own goals, in concert with the overall financial goals of the institution.

The Board's Role

The board of directors also plays an important role in the implementation of the development plan, so they should be included in the planning process as well. As with the CEO, the board will be involved in cultivation and solicitation of donors, as well as identifying potential donors for the organization. Therefore, they must be involved in setting realistic goals for major gifts received, number of calls made, and so on. Likewise, they also need to be aware of the costs of implementing the plan. Often board members do not realize that "it takes money to make money." Having them involved in the planning process will result in their buy-in and should also serve to help create enthusiasm for getting involved in the fundraising activities of the organization.

The board's role in developing the plan should be investigated before the development office begins the process. What has been the board's previous involvement in fundraising and in developing the plan? Who are the key players on the board who can be helpful in both the development and the implementation of the plan? Is there a development committee of the board?

In contrast to organizations that have been successful in implementing their plans, those who report that they were not as successful as they would like to have been report that a great part of their failure was not including the board in the planning process. A smaller organization reports that energizing the board and getting their involvement was difficult because they were not involved in the planning process and setting goals. Although board members were involved in calling donors with whom they had a personal connection to thank them for their gifts, they were uncomfortable with identifying, cultivating, and soliciting new donors.

These are key questions to ask before determining the involvement level of board and volunteers.

The Development Committee

All organizations involved in fundraising should have a group of volunteers, chaired by a board member and with several board members, along with other volunteers, who will serve as the development committee. This committee can be named the committee on philanthropy, the development council, the development committee, the fundraising committee, or any number of other titles. A brainstorming session with the core committee members can be helpful in choosing a name that suits the organization. Some organizations prefer using the word *philanthropy* instead of *development*. Particularly in a geographic area that is rapidly growing, the word *development* may be associated more with building and construction or real estate development, so it may confuse participants being invited to serve on that committee. *Philanthropy* implies a broader scope than either *development* or *fundraising*. In fact, Kay Sprinkel Grace uses the following example to show the depth of the philanthropic world:

Interrelationship of Values-Based Philanthropy, Development, and Fund raising

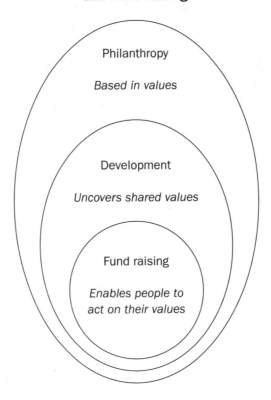

Philanthropy

Based in values

Development

Uncovers shared values

Fund raising

Enables people to act on their values

Grace goes on to say that the "mastery of the interrelationship of values-based philanthropy, development, and fundraising is a critical achievement for organizations seeking innovative and powerful ways to position themselves in their communities," and that "the integration of these functions is the primary premise in going beyond fundraising." Development and fundraising should always be set in the greater context of philanthropy. Philanthropy must be the guiding force of the development plan, and development professionals must always keep in mind that their greatest obligation is to the donor, then to the institution, and finally to themselves as professionals. The development office and the organization as a whole must also remember that development is about building relationships, and the development plan will need to include many aspects that aren't strictly "fundraising," such as cultivation and public awareness strategies, stewardship, research, and the like, all of which are important development strategies that do not involve actual fundraising.

The development committee, perhaps more than any entity outside of the CDO, will take a leading role in the development planning process. Depending on the size and strength of the development office staff, the development committee will fill a role that ranges from developing the entire plan (where there is no development staff) or approving the plan goals, objectives, and strategies, to implementing the plan. In most cases, the development committee will establish the goals and strategies along with the staff; and staff will develop the actions steps, timelines, and budget for the plan. However, the development committee can often be helpful in developing these items as well, particularly if they have a lot of experience with fundraising, either with this organization or with others. In *Recruiting and Training Fundraising Volunteers* (Lysakowski), there are several tips on finding the right people to serve on the development committee and involving them in the planning process.

Finding the right people to serve on the development committee has been a serious challenge for many development officers. The development office must first define the role of the development committee and determine how much of this role will involve the planning process. In some larger organizations, where there is sufficient staff to do the planning and the level of the volunteers is such that they are not interested in the details of the philanthropic process, this committee may focus more on implementing the plan than on developing it. Some organizations, for example, have a committee on philanthropy, whose role is limited to identification, cultivation, and solicitation of donors. For other organizations, especially where there is limited staff, the development committee may take a more active role in planning events, doing research, performing public relations functions, and development planning. Many smaller organizations that do not have a development staff or have a staff limited to one person, perhaps with little expertise in fundraising, can benefit from involving development officers from larger organizations who are willing to assume a more active role in the planning process. In fact, many smaller organizations have successfully recruited development professionals from their local universities and hospitals to serve on their development committees with this express intent in mind. Recognizing that there would be a conflict of interest on the part of these development officers to raise money for an organization other than their own, the smaller organizations have successfully recruited highly experienced and well-respected development officers to provide advice, help with the planning process, and other nonsoliciting roles, such as the development of a case for support.

Consultants

Many organizations engage a consultant to help with their development plan, especially if the organization is new to fundraising, has limited staff, or has no development committee. One of the principal benefits of using consulting help is that the consultant will be able to help the organization establish realistic goals and objectives. The consultant will also be a good impartial judge of the organization's expectations in fulfilling the goals and can recommend tools to help implement the plan, such as a software system, research techniques, and board and staff training.

Finding the right consultant, like finding the right staff or board members, is an important step in the process. Some organizations find that issuing a request for proposal (RFP) is the best way to find a consultant that meets their needs. Others may have a consultant with whom they have previously worked, perhaps on a capital campaign, and with whom they feel comfortable. In this case, they can expedite the process by engaging a consultant whose work style and product they are already familiar with. If the organization plans to issue an RFP, they may want to start by narrowing the field of consultants to whom they will send the RFP. Sometimes geographic considerations are the principal factor in selecting a pool of consultants to choose from, particularly if travel expenses will strain the budget. For other organizations, the top priority may be to find a consultant who has worked with similar organizations, for example, hospitals, art museums, etc. One factor that should always be a criterion is the level of experience this consultant has with preparing development plans. Although that sounds like an obvious statement, many organizations get so wrapped up in considering the number of similar organizations the consultant has worked with, that they don't question what *type* of work this consultant has done with the other organizations. A consultant who specializes in board development or grant writing, for example, may have never had the experience of writing a complete development plan, so while his or her expertise will be helpful in a specific area or areas, he or she may not be the right consultant for *this* job. Ask to see samples of other plans he or she has done. Most consultants will have generic samples that do not violate the confidentiality of their clients.

If the organization does not have a list of consultants they wish to interview, they can start by asking other nonprofits who have done a development plan for the names of consultants with whom they have worked. They can also access a list of consultants who are Association of Fundraising Professionals (AFP) members through the AFP Web site at www.afpnet.org. There are numerous other local or regional associations of consultants that can be used as well. A search of the Internet may provide an initial list of consultants. Or, if there is a nonprofit center or association of nonprofits in the state or community, they may have consultant lists available as well. A checklist (Exhibit 2.1) to help select the right consultant is included at the end of this chapter.

If the organization does plan to work with a consultant to do their plan, it will be more efficient, and probably more economical, if the organization can prepare in advance for working with the consultant. A checklist of things to prepare for a development audit (Exhibit 3.1) is found at the end of Chapter 3.

IN THE REAL WORLD

One development officer reports that her experience in using a consultant helped tremendously because the consultant had a different view of the organization than anyone on the inside. He adapted fresh, new ideas that would work in her organization's culture and helped her present the development goals to the rest of the staff. In fact, this development officer used the knowledge she gained from working with the consultant to help her develop her own plan in a future job with another organization.

This form will be helpful to assess the organization's past fundraising performance, even if they are not planning to do a full-blown development audit. This information will be helpful in educating the consultant about the organization's past fundraising activities.

Summary

The CDO plays the lead role in preparing the development plan, including determining who else needs to be involved, when the plan will be done, and scheduling planning meetings. This role should also include evaluating the past performance of the development program or, where there is no past fundraising program to evaluate, assess the organization's readiness to do fundraising.

Other development staff, in cases where there is a staffed development department, should be involved with establishing the goals and objectives and in developing strategies that are workable. Staff members should particularly understand the plan for their areas of responsibility.

The CEO must be involved in establishing goals and needs to understand and commit the resources needed to implement the plan. For this reason, it is also wise to include the CFO in the planning process. Other non-development staff members that can be particularly helpful are the program department heads, who can become real allies for the development office when they are included in the planning process.

The board should also be involved in setting goals and must understand the part they will play in implementing the plan. If the board is not involved in the planning process, it is highly unlikely they will participate in making it happen.

The development committee, in particular, will be helpful in developing the plan, presenting the plan to the board, and implementing the plan. In smaller organizations where staff is limited, their role may be much greater than in a larger organization that has staff to do most of the planning. The development committee chair is generally the best person to present the plan to the board because they are peers.

Some organizations engage a consultant to help them with the plan, especially if this is the first plan they have done, if the staff time is limited, or if they want an objective evaluation of their past performance.

Further Reading

Allison, Michael, and Jude Kaye. *Strategic Planning for Nonprofit Organizations* (New York: John Wiley & Sons, 1997).

Sprinkel Grace, Kay. *Beyond Fundraising* (New York: John Wiley & Sons, 1997).

Lysakowski, Linda. *Recruiting and Training Fundraising Volunteers* (Hoboken, N.J.: John Wiley & Sons, 2005).

EXHIBIT 2.1

Selecting a Consultant Checklist

☐ *Determine that outside help is needed.* Identify problem and achieve board/staff consensus that a consultant is needed.

☐ *Select the appropriate type of consultant.* Understand the specific type of services needed and types of professionals that are available; determine budget.

☐ *Identify possible consultants.* Ask for referrals from colleagues, professional organizations.

☐ *Make initial contact with possible consultants.* Call, make notes of initial reaction, verify availability, narrow the list to three or four firms.

☐ *Provide information about your organization.* Ask what information they need, determine whether you will meet with this consultant in person.

☐ *Design interviews with consultants.* Determine who in your organization will make the final hiring decision, how many firms will you interview, how much time will you allow for each interview, who will be involved, and what questions will you ask.

☐ *Conduct initial interviews.* Assess consultant's understanding of your organization's needs, determine if their style and personality will fit your organization, obtain information on fees and expenses, ask for references, and request a written proposal.

☐ *Receive and review proposals.* Determine if the proposals meet your guidelines; check references; determine importance of personality, experience, approach, and costs; select finalists.

☐ *Have finalists make presentation to board, committee, and/or executive staff.* Provide interviewers with information beforehand, guide discussion to pertinent questions, and assess consultant's ability to command board/staff's interest, attention, and respect.

- *Make decision.* Inform the firm of your final choice and set up meeting to negotiate contract.

- *Don't notify your second, third, or fourth choices until your contract is signed* in case your first-choice consultant is not available or contract negotiations fail.

- *Welcome consultant to your organization* and introduce them to key staff with whom they will be working.

CHAPTER 3

Planning to Plan

"Men [and women] who love wisdom should acquaint themselves
with a great many particulars."
Heraclitus

After reading this chapter, you will be able to:

- Develop a schedule for the planning process.
- Prepare for the planning process.
- List components of a development audit.
- Evaluate past performance of the development program.

When Should the Organization Do a Development Plan?

When does the organization need a development plan? All organizations should have a development plan, but it is particularly vital for the organization or the development officer new to fundraising. Development positions have one of the highest rates of turnover in the nonprofit world. Currently, the average length of time a development officer remains in his or her position is approximately two years. One reason is believed to be that development officers are often faced with unrealistic expectations from their chief executive officer (CEO) and board.

Another reason for high turnover is that many development officers are simply worn out from planning too many events. One of the most common mistakes of boards and senior staff members who do not have an understanding of how development works is to jump on the event bandwagon. Let's face it—events are easy to do even if the organization has no history of fundraising and no donor base. Almost every organization has someone who is a good party planner, and so the organization gets drawn into the bottomless pit of special events—walkathons, runs, galas, casino nights, the list goes on and on.

Lilya Wagner states that the reasons for the high stress level in the development office are:

- They must deal with a variety of people on a daily basis—donors, staff members, volunteers, media, board, and volunteers.

- Unrealistic goals imposed by board or management.

- Lack of training and mentoring.

- Board members' lack of follow-through on promises, and attitudes of "I'll do anything but fundraise."

- Inadequate budgets for development.

- Inadequate support staff.

- General lack of understanding of the profession of fundraising.

All of these must be addressed in the development plan. Wagner further states that professionals should be on the alert for the signs that indicate they have been placed in a no-win situation. These signs include:

- Fundraising is a low priority for the organization.

- The development office is out of the loop within the organizational hierarchy.

- Important information is withheld from the development office.

- There is no prospect base.

- There is an imbalance between planned gifts and cash gifts.

- The board is not involved in fundraising.

- The development department is expected to work miracles.

Wagner states that in an effort to relieve the stresses of the development office, there are several helpful tools, the first of which is to "be a good planner." She also lists setting realistic goals and being a team player, all of which can be addressed by ensuring that there is a development plan in place.

The development plan can be an excellent tool for development officers who want to remain in the profession, relieve stress on themselves, and are committed to advancing the mission of their organization. Other critical reasons to consider a development plan are discussed next.

When the Organization Is Preparing for a Capital Campaign

An organization preparing for any major endeavor such as a capital campaign or major-gift initiative should be sure it has an integrated development plan that includes goals and objectives for its annual fund as well as these new projects. Often, during a capital campaign, the annual fund gets shortchanged while the organization focuses on the campaign. This can be very dangerous, as the annual fund is important for several reasons. Not only do most organizations count on the income from the annual fund to cover operating expenses, but the annual fund is the primary cultivation ground for major gifts. Donors need to be made aware of the need for ongoing support as well as special project funding. The annual fund can be a good foundation for the capital campaign, and, conversely, the capital campaign often identifies and solidifies relationships with donors who have now made a major commitment. Most organizations do not take full advantage of their capital campaign experience to build a strong bond with donors. The development plan should include strategies to ensure that these donors are kept on the radar screen for future annual gifts as well as major and planned gifts. It will be important to have a strong case for support for the annual campaign and other fundraising projects and to include all aspects of the fundraising program in the development plan.

Organizational Strategic Planning

Another good time to do the development plan is when the organization is involved in a strategic planning process. An overall organizational plan should include a program plan, a facilities plan, a human resources plan, and a financial development plan. For many organizations, the time to do their long-range development plan is during the strategic planning process for the organization. It will be important to incorporate the development plan into the overall plan so the expectations for raising money to meet growing program, staffing, and/or facility needs are not out of line with what is realistic from the development standpoint.

New Staff

Many organizations place a greater emphasis on development planning when new development staff is brought on board. Once a new person is hired, especially if this is the first person in a development position, they will want to start by evaluating past performance or the organization's readiness for fundraising and then immediately develop a strategy to ensure that there is a plan in place for the development office. The new development officer must have a plan to work with, so if there is already one in place when they are hired, they may just need to review it and possibly update it. If there has been a gap between development officers, it is likely that some of the steps in the plan have fallen by the wayside while the organization was attempting to fill the vacant position. If there is no plan in place, this is the perfect opportunity for the development officer to get off on the right foot by ensuring that they have a plan from which to work.

Sometimes a new CEO will request that a new plan be done or, at a minimum, that he or she is in agreement with the goals of the existing plan. So, when a new CEO comes on board, the chief development officer (CDO) should make it a priority to meet with the CEO and review the current plan. The two of them can then decide if the goals and objectives are still appropriate and the development office can make revisions as needed.

Renewed Board Involvement

Often, the board is the impetus behind getting a development plan in place. Particularly when new board members are appointed who have served on other boards for organizations that have had a strong development plan, this will be the case. Or the board may have new leadership that will request renewed or new involvement of the board in fundraising. When this is the case, the development officer can be assured that the board will buy into the plan.

What Is Needed to Get Started?
Consensus that a Plan Is Needed

First, the organization needs buy-in from the management and board. Many development officers have spent a lot of time working on plans that never get implemented because resources are not available or board members are not willing to take part in the fundraising program. A CEO who is committed to development will not only encourage, but also will require the CDO to prepare an annual plan and will review the plan with the development officer on a regular basis. This is an excellent tool for performance evaluation time. The CDO should be prepared to discuss the plan and their progress in implementing each objective during his or her evaluation interview. Likewise, other development staff persons should be prepared to discuss their sections of the plan when the CDO does his or her annual performance review.

Past Development Results

Another necessary tool will be reports on past years' performance. Some forms are found at the end of this chapter to evaluate the development office's past performance (Exhibits 3.1, 3.2, and 3.3). These tools will help the development office and/or the consultant assess strengths and weaknesses of the development office. Some areas to look at are growth (or decline) in numbers of donors, number of dollars raised through each fundraising method, amount of average gift, number of volunteer fundraisers involved, percentage of the board who made a gift, and percentage of staff who made a gift. Other helpful statistics include the size of the board, the involvement of the board in fundraising, the number of people serving on the development committee, the number of publications produced, the number of donor contacts made during the year, and the number of major gift calls made per month. An evaluation of each special event should also be performed to determine if this event should be continued or eliminated. A form is found at the end of this chapter to assess special events (Exhibit 3.4). Also, the number of grant proposals that have been successfully funded should be assessed.

SWOT Analysis

A helpful exercise is to take the development staff through a SWOT Analysis. SWOT stands for strengths, weaknesses, opportunities, and threats. The development staff and/or the development committee should evaluate the last year's results, compared to goals that were established. This will help ensure that unrealistic goals are not being established for the year ahead. The organization may have gone through an overall SWOT analysis during a strategic planning process, but this SWOT analysis will focus solely on the development office. A meeting should be set aside towards the end of each fiscal year for this purpose. If the organization has not gone through a SWOT analysis before, some things to keep in mind follow.

 TIPS & TECHNIQUES

The SWOT Analysis

- Remember that strengths and weaknesses are internal to the organization; opportunities and threats are external influences that may affect the plan.

- Some items may fall into more than one category; for example, a strength might be that the organization has a donor software package that is able to generate accurate reports and donor entries. This same item may be a weakness if there is no staff trained in using the software, or if bad data has been entered into the system.

- Participants in the process must be honest about weaknesses and threats; sometimes these are difficult to discuss.

- A good facilitator will be needed to help participants focus only on things that relate to the development plan.

- The results of the SWOT analysis will change each year, but if a consistent weakness is listed year after year, steps must be taken to address this weakness.

Budgets

Another key need before attempting to develop the plan is budgets—both the organizational budget itself and the development office budget. It will be important for the development officer both to have access to and understand the overall budget for the organization. This is important for several reasons. First, it will help the development office understand the needs of the organization for which they will be raising the money. Second, the development office should be aware of any financial restraints the organization may have that will affect the development office, such as a freeze on hiring, plans to update organization-wide software systems, adding new programs, and so on.

One of the biggest budgeting mistakes made by nonprofits, especially those new to the fundraising arena, is to establish a fundraising goal for the development office simply by looking at the organization's overall budget, deducting the anticipated income from the anticipated expenses, and saying to the development office, "Okay, here is the deficit, go raise the money to cover it." Establishing fundraising goals is a much more complex process and *must* involve the development office.

Another misguided approach to goal setting is to look at similar-sized organizations and determine the fundraising goal based on what these other organizations are raising. There are many factors that go into establishing a reasonable fundraising goal. Among these factors are the past fundraising history of the organization, the number of natural prospective donors available (alumni, grateful patients, parents, etc.), the infrastructure in place (software systems, etc.), the level of involvement of the board, the size of the development office staff, the level of experience of development staff members, and the level of public awareness about the organization and its programs.

The management of the organization must both invite and trust the development officer's judgment in establishing goals for the development office. Development goals should also include some nonfinancial goals, such as number of donors visited per month, number of increased donations, and percentage of involvement of specific prospect groups such as alumni.

Time

Time is another factor to consider. A good plan takes time to develop, and staff and board must be willing to set aside time to develop a plan. For organizations whose fiscal year ends June 30, summer is often a good time to plan, as things tend to be slower then. Most organizations are not doing a tremendous amount of mailings, events, and the like during the summer. For those whose fiscal year ends December 31, the same thing can apply to the end of the year "slowdown." Although year-end is a busy time for some organizations, especially in the planned giving or direct mail areas, there is often a lull from the middle of November through the end of the year when the plan can be developed or updated.

The organization must consider the time schedules of those who will be involved—if there are vacations to consider, holidays to be accommodated, and so on. Particularly if board members and other volunteers will be involved, the staff needs to be sensitive to the time constraints of volunteers and plan accordingly.

How Long Will It Take to Develop the Plan?

The process will be longer for some organizations and shorter for others, but typically the plan takes about three months to develop from start to finish. As Allison and Kaye point out, though, sometimes even an organizational strategic plan must be done in a shorter period of time, and the development officer who is faced with a crisis situation may be asked to produce a plan within a few days. If this is the first plan the organization has done, it will most likely take a full three months to complete, considering time for the evaluation and assessment of the current situation. Once the plan is in place, annual updates may take a month or less, depending on how many new initiatives are to be undertaken during the upcoming year. The plan should not be viewed as a static document, written in stone. It should be a vital, living document that is assessed on a regular basis and adjusted as necessary, so in some ways it is never really finished.

What Time Frame Does the Plan Cover?

A good development plan has both short- and long-term goals. Often, the strategies and action steps will be more detailed in the shorter-term goals. The long-term goals are generally more fluid, as circumstances may change before these steps are implemented. Most strategic planning experts agree that three to five years is a good time frame for long-range goals, whereas short-term goals are generally thought of as one-year goals. In the development office, there should always be an annual work plan that serves to help the department plan its day-to-day activities. However, long-range goals are important, too. If, for example, the organization anticipates a capital campaign three or four years from now, or even longer, there are some planning steps that need to be in place long before the campaign actually gets launched.

Once a solid plan is in place, it must be revisited on an annual basis. Circumstances most often change from year to year. It may be that the economy and/or the demographics of the community have changed and the development function may need to adapt to these changes. It may be that staff turnover has allowed some of the action steps to fall through the cracks, and for this reason a monthly or, at the very least, quarterly benchmarking by the development department will ensure that the plan is kept on track. If the plan is working, perhaps only minor changes will be needed for the following year.

The Development Audit

Often, the first step in development planning is for the organization to do a full-blown development audit. For organizations that are new to development, an audit is usually not required, although the organization would want to evaluate its resources through some of the methods suggested in the preceding sections of this Book. But for larger organizations that have a track record of development activities, an audit can be helpful in determining what areas need improvement.

Like a financial audit, a development audit should be done by an outside consultant who can look objectively at the organization and compare it with other organizations of similar size and scope and analyze its results based on acceptable standards for the profession. A development audit is an internal assessment of the organization's fundraising program and its readiness to embark on new development ventures. The development audit looks at involvement of board, staff, and volunteers in the fundraising process and offers recommendations on how to best use the human resources available to the organization. All of these recommendations will be helpful when the organization embarks on the development planning process. The audit evaluates the strengths and weaknesses of the organization's development systems, including fundraising software. The audit also offers suggestions to help improve donor communications and stewardship.

TIPS & TECHNIQUES

Many organizations consider a development audit when they are:

- Preparing to embark on a major-gift, capital, or endowment campaign.

- Not satisfied with the results of their annual giving program.

- Seeking to increase board participation in fundraising efforts.

- Attempting to compare their results with similar organizations.

- Looking for an objective evaluation their development program.

- Trying to diversify their funding streams.

- Engaged in the strategic planning process.

- Looking at restructuring their development office.

- Seeking to take their program to a higher level of professionalism.

In most cases, the audit is done by a consultant in order to gain both objectivity and utilize the knowledge and years of experience the consultant will bring to the table. The staff, while not involved directly in the evaluation process, will need to devote time to the audit process. Typical staff roles include:

- Completion of development audit questionnaires.

- Providing supporting documentation.

- Meeting with the consultant to clarify information and set goals for the audit.

The board is also generally involved with the process, completing questionnaires and participating in interviews with the consultant. Typically, the board chair, chair of the development committee, and other selected board members will be involved in interviews. The consultant will usually make several visits to the organization to meet with key staff, board, and other volunteers.

A development audit will look at these areas:

- The organization's readiness for fundraising:
  - *Legal structure.* Does the organization have 501(c)3 status or other appropriate Governmental Recognition as a Charitable organization?
  - *Organizational structure.* To whom does the chief development officer report?
  - *Strategic planning.* Does the organization have a long-range plan?
  - *Fundraising guidelines.* Are there gift acceptance policies in place?
  - *Case for support.* Is there a written organizational case for support and case statements to support various fundraising needs?

- The board's role in fundraising:
  - *Board composition.* Is the board diverse, and does it have the appropriate mix of skills and talents?
  - *Board performance.* Is the board actively involved in fundraising, and do board members support the organization financially?

48

○ *The development committee.* Is there a development committee or other volunteers involved in the fundraising program?

- The role of staff:

  ○ *Departmental structure.* Is there adequate staff, doing the right jobs with the right tools?

  ○ *Functions of the development office.* Does the development staff have the time and skills to perform all development functions?

  ○ *Training and educating staff.* Is there a commitment to professionalism in the development office?

  ○ *Role of the CEO in fundraising.* Is the CEO involved in fundraising and does he/she communicate regularly with the development office?

- Systems and procedures:

  ○ *Donor database software.* Is there an adequate donor software program in place, and is staff trained to use the program?

  ○ *Procedure manual.* Are there procedures in place to receive, record, and acknowledge gifts?

  ○ *Hardware.* Is there adequate hardware to support development systems and programs?

  ○ *Internet usage and Web site.* Does staff use technology to improve donor relations?

- Cultivation and stewardship:

  ○ *Prospect research.* Are adequate time and resources committed to donor/prospect research?

  ○ *Cultivation strategies.* Is there a program in place to build donor relationships?

  ○ *Communications.* How does the organization communicate with its various publics?

- ○ *Acknowledgment.* Are donors thanked in a timely manner?

- ○ *Recognition.* Is adequate donor recognition given?

- The integrated development program—does the organization rely too heavily on one source of funding or is there a plan in place to develop funding from various sources, including:

  - ○ Grants

  - ○ Special events

  - ○ Direct mail

  - ○ Telephone fundraising

  - ○ Major gifts

  - ○ Corporate appeals

  - ○ Planned gifts

Once the development audit is complete, the report should be used to develop a strategic plan for development, addressing the areas raised as issues needing improvement in the audit. A comprehensive development audit can help an organization build on its strengths, overcome its weaknesses, and address opportunities for future growth. A checklist to help prepare for a development audit (Exhibit 3.5) is found at the end of this chapter.

One organization, preparing for its first development audit, chose a consultant who had done audits for similar-sized organizations but had not worked with an organization in their field before. However, the chemistry between the CDO and the consultant was good, and they felt this would be a productive working relationship.

The consultant interviewed numerous people within the organization, including the CEO, the chief financial officer (CFO), the human resources director, the public relations director, and other development staff. The organization was going through an audit of all its functions simultaneously—human resources, finances, and program—so the development audit was understood by the organization to be an important part of this process, leading to continuous quality improvement.

The audit showed several strengths that the organization felt it could build on, especially in the major-gift area. Some of its weaknesses, such as understaffing and technology gaps, were addressed during the audit, which provided them a guideline for improving production in the developmental office.

As a result of the audit, the organization developed a moves management system to focus the chief development officer's time on major donors and freed up her time by shifting some of her duties to other development staff people.

Summary

Nonprofit organizations should do a development plan on an annual basis. However, it is critical that a plan be done when the organization is contemplating a capital campaign or some other major endeavor, if they are in the process of doing an organizational strategic plan, if new development staff has been hired, when the board is expected to assume a greater role in funding, or when a new CEO is on board.

A development plan should include both short-term goals (one year) and long-range goals (three to five years). The full plan generally takes about three months to prepare, but if a development audit has been done or some other evaluation process has already taken place, the time frame may be shorter. If a full plan has been done and it just needs updating on an annual basis, it will probably take a month or so to complete the update, again depending on how much analysis has been done or needs to be done. For organizations new to development, there usually is not much to analyze, but the organization should still assess its readiness to take on new fundraising efforts.

There are several things that must be in place before the plan can be started:

- Consensus on the part of the board and executive management that a plan is needed and will be implemented.

- Budgets for the organization and the development office.

- A planning committee.

- Time to do the analysis and goal setting for the development office.

- A SWOT analysis of the development office.

- An evaluation of past performance, either through a development audit or an internal assessment of the development program.

Further Reading

Wagner, Lilya. *Careers in Fundraising* (Hoboken, N.J.: John Wiley & Sons, 2002).

Allison, Michael, and Jude Kaye. *Strategic Planning for Nonprofit Organizations* (New York: John Wiley & Sons, 1997).

Evaluating Your Development Program

Organization
Name _____

	2 points	1 point	0 points
1. Our organization has 501(c)3 or other Charitable tax status.	Yes	Pending	No
2. We have a sufficient number of members on our board of directors. Number of board members ____	Yes	In process	No
3. There is staff devoted exclusively to development. Number of development staff ____	Yes	In process	No
4. We have a nonprofit bulk rate permit.	Yes	Pending	No
5. We are registered with the state regulatory authority if required.	Yes	Pending	No
6. We have an organizational strategic plan.	Yes	In process	No
7. We have a mission written statement.	Yes	In process	No
8. We have a vision written statement.	Yes	In process	No
9. We have a long-range development plan.	Yes	In process	No
10. We are on track with our development plan.	Yes	In process	No
11. We have gift acceptance policies in place.	Yes	In process	No
12. Our staff and volunteers are familiar with and follow these policies.	Yes	Somewhat	No
13. We have a written organizational case for support.	Yes	In process	No
14. We have written case statements for each component of our development program.	Yes	In process	No

continued on the next page

	2 points	1 point	0 points
15. Our board is comprised of a good mix of diverse backgrounds.	Yes	In process	No
16. Our board has skills and talents needed by our organization.	Yes	Some	No
17. Our board has influence and affluence.	Yes	Some	No
18. Our board members understand their role.	Yes	Some	No
19. Our board is actively involved in our development efforts.	Yes	Some	No
20. Our board members contribute financially.	Yes	Some	No
21. Our board has active committees.	Yes	In process	No
22. We have an active development committee.	Yes	In process	No
23. We have sufficient staff assigned to development activities.	Yes	In process	No
24. Our chief development officer reports directly to the CEO.	Yes		No
25. Our development office interfaces with and has good relations with other departments.	Yes	Some	No
26. We have appropriate people assigned to various development functions.	Yes	Some	No
27. We hold productive staff meetings for the development staff on a regular basis.	Yes	Some	No
28. Our development staff is active in AFP and/or other professional organizations.	Yes	Some	No
29. Our staff receives development education on a regular basis.	Yes	Some	No
30. Our staff members are cross-trained to fill all development functions.	Yes	Some	No
31. Our staff members have appropriate educational backgrounds.	Yes	Some	No
32. The CEO supports development efforts.	Yes	Sometimes	No

	2 points	1 point	0 points
33. The CEO provides good management and is respected in the community.	Yes	Somewhat	No
34. The CEO is involved with cultivation and solicitation of donors.	Yes	Sometimes	No
35. We have a donor database that performs all the necessary development functions.	Yes	In process	No
36. We have a procedure manual in place.	Yes	In process	No
37. We have all the necessary office equipment, i.e., laser printers, computers, etc.	Yes	In process	No
38. We are online and use email to communicate with doners and volunteers.	Yes	In process	No
39. Our staff is able to prioritize their development functions to spend appropriate time on each.	Yes	Some	No
40. We have a research program in place using electronic and informal research.	Yes	In process	No
41. We hold regular cultivation events.	Yes	In process	No
42. We communicate well with donors/ prospects through printed media— brochures, newsletters, annual reports.	Yes	Some	No
43. We issue press releases regularly.	Yes	Some	No
44. We have an organization video.	Yes	In process	No
45. We have an effective Web site.	Yes	In process	No
46. We acknowledge gifts within 24 hours.	Yes	Usually	No
47. We send personal thank-you notes in addition to official receipts.	Yes	Sometimes	No
48. We call "major" donors to thank them.	Yes	Sometimes	No
49. We list donors in our annual report and/or newsletters.	Yes	Some	No
50. We have regular donor recognition events.	Yes	Some	No
51. We have a giving club program.	Yes	In process	No

continued on the next page

	2 points	1 point	0 points
52. We offer appropriate naming opportunities for major/capital gifts.	Yes	In process	No
53. We have a planned giving program in place.	Yes	In process	No
54. We have an endowment fund.	Yes	In Process	No
55. We set goals realistically.	Yes	Somewhat	No
56. We regularly assess the performance of special events.	Yes	Sometimes	No
57. We effectively use volunteers for special events.	Yes	Sometimes	No
58. We spend 90% of our time working with the top 10% of our donors.	Yes	Somewhat	No
59. Our development staff feels they are making a valuable contribution to the organization.	Yes	Some	No
60. Our board members and volunteers feel good about their fundraising efforts.	Yes	Some	No
Total Score:	_____ @ 2 Points = _____	_____ @ 1 Points = _____	_____ @ 0 Points = _____
Score question 61:	**80 points**	**40 points**	**0 points**
61. We have an integrated approach to development	Yes	In process	No
Development Program	Current Year	Last Year	Previous Years
Grants Received			
Special Events			
Direct Mail			
Telephone Solicitation			
Personal Solicitation			
Total Score of Questions 1–60			
Total Score of Question 61			
Grand Total			

176–200 Points	Your development program is excellent
151–175 Points	Your program is strong and effective
126–150 Points	You need to improve on some areas of your program
101–125 Points	Many of the areas of your program need to be improved
51–100 Points	You need some serious work on your development program
Under 50 Points	You need to totally restructure your development program

EXHIBIT 3.2

Quick and Easy Development Audit Form

Organization
Name: _____

We have a completed, written mission statement.	____Yes ____No ____In process
We have a completed, written vision statement.	____Yes ____No ____In process
We have an organizational long-range plan.	____Yes ____No ____In process
We have a development department and long-range and short-range plans.	____Yes ____No ____In process
We have a completed, written case statement.	____Yes ____No ____In process
We have written, approved gift acceptance policies.	____Yes ____No ____In process
We have a development procedure manual.	____Yes ____No ____In process
We have 501(c)3 or other tax-exempt status.	____Yes ____No ____In process
We have met state registration requirements.	____Yes ____No ____In process
Number on board of directors____ Term limits	____Yes ____No
Operating committees?	____Yes ____No ____Not effective
The board understands their role in the organization.	____Yes ____No ____Some

The board contributes   ____100% ____75% ____50%
    financially.   ____25% or less

The board is involved in fundraising.   ____Yes ____No ____Some

We do special appeals/events for
major donors.   ____Yes ____No

We have giving clubs.   ____Yes ____No

We have donor recognition events/programs.   ____Yes ____No

We have volunteer recognition events/programs. ____Yes ____No

We have a prospect research program in place. ____Yes ____No

We have a planned giving program in place.   ____Yes ____No

We have a donor cultivation program in place.   ____Yes ____No

Gifts are acknowledged within ____24–48 hrs. of receipt ____48 hrs.–1 wk.
____1 wk. or longer ____Only over the amount of $____   ____ Not at all

We have fundraising software.   ____Yes ____No Type____

We have staff trained to use this software   ____Yes ____No
to its full capacity.   ____Somewhat

We have sufficient hardware, including
laser printers.   ____Yes ____No

We effectively use e-mail to communicate   ____Yes ____No
    with staff Donors and Volunteers

We have an effective Web site.   ____Yes ____No

We publish the following: ___Annual report   ___Brochures ___Newsletter
                    ___ Press releases ___ Other _____

Total dollars raised last year $ _____

continued on the next page

Funding Area	Group	Personal Visits	Phone	Mail	Events	Grants
Annual: Total Raised $						
	Corporate	$	$	$	$	$
	Individual	$	$	$	$	$
	Foundations	$	$	$	$	$
	Organizations	$	$	$	$	$
Capital: Total Raised $						
	Corporate	$	$	$	$	$
	Individual	$	$	$	$	$
	Foundations	$	$	$	$	$
	Organizations	$	$	$	$	$
Endowment: Total Raised $						
	Corporate	$	$	$	$	$
	Individual	$	$	$	$	$
	Foundations	$	$	$	$	$
	Organizations	$	$	$	$	$
Other: Total Raised $						
	Corporate	$	$	$	$	$
	Individual	$	$	$	$	$
	Foundations	$	$	$	$	$
	Organizations	$	$	$	$	$

EXHIBIT 3.3

Development Planning Worksheet

_____ Organization

Overall Fundraising Goal $ _____ for Fiscal Year _____

Membership	Last Yr Total	Goal Year 1	Goal Year 2	Goal Year 3
Member count	#	#	#	#
Total dollars raised	$	$	$	$
Resources available:				
Issues to overcome:				
Strategies:				
Target date:		Coordinator Assigned:		
Committee:				

Event 1	Last Yr Total	Goal Year 1	Goal Year 2	Goal Year 3
Attendee count	#	#	#	#
Total dollars raised	$	$	$	$
Resources available:				
Issues to overcome:				
Strategies:				
Target date:		Coordinator assigned:		
Committee:				

continued on the next page

Event 2	Last Yr Total	Goal Year 1	Goal Year 2	Goal Year 3
Attendee count	#	#	#	#
Total dollars raised	$	$	$	$
Resources available:				
Issues to overcome:				
Strategies:				
Target date:		Coordinator assigned:		
Committee:				

Event 3	Last Yr Total	Goal Year 1	Goal Year 2	Goal Year 3
Attendee count	#	#	#	#
Total dollars raised	$	$	$	$
Resources available:				
Issues to overcome:				
Strategies:				
Target date:		Coordinator assigned:		
Committee:				

Special	Last Yr Total	Goal Year 1	Goal Year 2	Goal Year 3
Attendee count	#	#	#	#
Total dollars raised	$	$	$	$
Resources available:				
Issues to overcome:				
Strategies:				
Target date:		Coordinator assigned:		
Committee:				

Foundation Grants	Last Yr Total	Goal Year 1	Goal Year 2	Goal Year 3
Number of grants awarded	#	#	#	#
Total dollars raised	$	$	$	$
Resources available:				
Issues to overcome:				
Strategies:				
Target date:		Coordinator assigned:		
Committee:				

continued on the next page

Corporate Appeal	Last Yr Total	Goal Year 1	Goal Year 2	Goal Year 3
Number of gifts received	#	#	#	#
Total dollars raised	$	$	$	$
Resources available:				
Issues to overcome:				
Strategies:				
Target date:		Coordinator Assigned:		
Committee:				

Major/Planned Gifts	Last Yr Total	Goal Year 1	Goal Year 2	Goal Year 3
Number of gifts received	#	#	#	#
Total dollars raised	$	$	$	$
Resources available:				
Issues to overcome:				
Strategies:				
Target date:		Coordinator assigned:		
Committee:				

Board Giving	Last Yr Total	Goal Year 1	Goal Year 2	Goal Year 3
Total # board members	#	#	#	#
Number of gifts received	#	#	#	#
Total dollars raised	$	$	$	$
Resources available:				
Issues to overcome:				
Strategies:				
Target date:		Coordinator assigned:		
Committee:				

Phone Appeal	Last Yr Total	Goal Year 1	Goal Year 2	Goal Year 3
Number of gifts received	#	#	#	#
Total dollars raised	$	$	$	$
Resources available:				
Issues to overcome:				
Strategies:				
Target date:		Coordinator assigned:		
Committee:				

continued on the next page

Mail Appeal	Last Yr Total	Goal Year 1	Goal Year 2	Goal Year 3
Number of gifts received	#	#	#	#
Total dollars raised	$	$	$	$
Resources available:				
Issues to overcome:				
Strategies:				
Target date:		Coordinator assigned:		
Committee:				

Capital Campaign	Last Capital Campaign	Goal Year 1	Goal Year 2	Goal Year 3
Number of gifts received	#	#	#	#
Total dollars raised	$	$	$	$
Resources available:				
Issues to overcome:				
Strategies:				
Target date:		Coordinator assigned:		
Committee:				

EXHIBIT 3.4

Special Events Evaluation

Name of Organization _____

Event _____

Purpose of Event: Fundraising _____ If yes, anticipated net proceeds $ _____

Friend raising _____ If yes, anticipated number people _____

Other _____

Strengths of this event: _____

_____

_____

_____

_____

Weaknesses of this event: _____

_____

_____

_____

_____

Ideas to make this event better: _____

_____

_____

_____

_____

_____

continued on the next page

Fundraising Activity	Date	Estimated Cost	Estimated Income	Est. Profit $000s	Staff Hours Req'd	Vol. Hours Req'd	New Names Acq'd	Taps Large Donors	Builds Aware-Ness	Risk Factor	Bonds Donors	Total	Ranking
					<25=5 25 – 100=3 100>=1	<100=5 100 – 200=3 200>=1	200+ =5 100 – 199=3 0–99=1	10+ =5 5–9=3 1–5=1	High=5 Med=3 Low=1	Low=5 Med=3 High=1	High=5 Med=3 Low=1		

Checklist for Development Audit

☐ Determine goals of audit

☐ Determine timeline and budget for audit

☐ Develop list of consultants to send RFP

☐ Develop and send RFP to consultants

☐ Accept proposals and select finalists

☐ Interview finalists

☐ Select consultant to do audit, check references and sign contract

☐ Establish final timeline with consultant

☐ Gather information for consultant:

    ○ List of board members with term expiration dates, committee assignments, and giving history

    ○ List of development committee members with term expiration dates, subcommittee assignments, and giving history

    ○ Staff organizational chart

    ○ Staff job descriptions

    ○ Board organizational chart

    ○ Board position descriptions

    ○ Long-range or strategic plan

    ○ Development plan

    ○ Bylaws

    ○ Mission statement

continued on the next page

○ Vision statement

○ Gift acceptance policies

○ Office procedure manual

○ Case for support

○ List of hardware and software used in development office

○ Copies of brochures used by development

○ Copies of annual report

○ Copies of newsletters

○ Campaign/appeal reports for past three years

○ Copies of appeal and acknowledgment letters

○ Copies of response envelopes and other collateral materials used by development office

○ Other information requested by the consultant

☐ Complete questionnaires or forms provided by consultant

☐ Prepare list of individuals to be interviewed by consultant

☐ Meet with consultant during various stages of audit

☐ Arrange interviews for consultant with selected staff, donors, board members, and volunteers

☐ Review draft of report

☐ Discuss with consultant the process for the presentation of the report

☐ Develop plan to implement recommendations from the report

CHAPTER 4

The Process

"Nine-tenths of wisdom consists in being wise in time."
Theodore Roosevelt

After reading this chapter, you will be able to:

- Determine who should be involved in the development planning process.
- List the information that will be needed for the plan.
- Set goals and objectives for the plan.
- Be able to establish areas of responsibilities, budgets, and timelines for the plan.

Once the organization has determined that it needs a development plan, one thing that is important to remember is that the process is just as important as the product. Deciding who will be involved; gathering the information; planning meetings; setting goals and objectives; and assigning timelines, responsibility, and budgets are all important steps and should not be overlooked. Often, the process of planning solidifies the development department relationships and helps promote a cohesive work atmosphere. So where to start?

Determining Who Will Be Involved

As mentioned in previous chapters, the size and scope of the development office will determine who will be involved in the development planning process. However, it should never be a one-person operation. A plan that was developed by one person will never receive buy-in from others whose help will be needed to implement the plan.

It is usually the chief development officer (CDO) who determines when the plan is needed and heads up the process. However, sometimes the CEO takes the lead and requests the plan from the development office at a certain time of the year. In cases where there is no development officer at all, the executive director or chair of the development committee may take the initiative to develop the plan. No matter what size development staff is available, there should always be one person who heads up the process and lays out the schedule. This person should begin by determining who needs to be involved.

The CEO should certainly have some involvement in goal setting and needs to be aware of the resources that will be needed by the development office, so there must be some involvement on the part of the CEO. The level of involvement will depend in great part on the size of the development staff and the personality of the CEO. Most executives do not want to—nor should they—be involved in the nitty-gritty details of the plan, but should certainly endorse the goals of the plan, so they will need to be brought in at some point early in the process. Another key non–development staff person who should be involved is the chief financial officer (CFO). In many organizations there is already tension between the finance office and the development office, so bringing the CFO in on the development planning process may serve the development office well by alleviating some of this tension.

The board should also be involved with the plan, at least to endorse the goals. Like the CEO, they will likely not get involved in the day-to-day details of the plan, but they can be helpful in setting the calendar because they will know the community and what other activities or major events other nonprofits may be

IN THE REAL WORLD

One organization that did not involve its board in the planning process lost a good development director because when she presented the finished plan to the board, they were shocked to find out that the development director expected them to assist with identifying and soliciting major donors. The board had not been previously involved with fundraising activities for the organization, and when the plan was presented to them with this expected involvement, they were blindsided. A heated discussion took place at the board meeting, resulting in the executive director's firing the development director to save herself from being embarrassed. The development officer had been new to this organization and had previously worked for an organization that had heavy board involvement, so she drew up a plan assuming that it would work at her new organization as successfully as it had at her previous place of employment.

doing that could conflict with the planned events of this organization. They also should be made aware of any activities that will require their involvement, such as identifying, cultivating, soliciting, and stewarding donors. If they are brought in early in the planning phase, they may also have some good suggestions for these activities that perhaps the development office had not previously considered.

Selecting who should be involved will be a critical first step in the planning process. At the end of this chapter are two charts (Exhibits 4.1 and 4.2) to help determine who will be involved and at what stage of the planning process they will be brought into the process.

Board and Volunteers

If the board has not previously been involved with the fundraising activities, it will be important to brief them at a board meeting about the goals of the plan and to get their buy-in for any aspects of the plan that require their involvement. The CDO should attend board meetings on a regular basis and, if it is not customary for him or her to make a report at board meetings, it will be beneficial for him or her to do so early in the planning process. This meeting can also be used to judge the level of commitment and enthusiasm for development on the part of individual board members. One or two board members who seem particularly interested in development activities can then be invited to serve on the planning committee. This meeting can also serve as an educational opportunity to provide some basic fundraising information and training for board members.

If there is a development committee, they will likely be more involved in the development of the plan than the board of directors will be. The development committee should devote a meeting at the end of each fiscal year to evaluating the past year's success and to establish goals for the coming year. Some members of the development committee might also be involved in the planning process and in presenting goals and objectives to the full board. It is generally better to have board members hear about their fundraising responsibilities from a peer than from staff.

TIPS & TECHNIQUES

The following persons should be invited to participate in the development planning process:

- CDO.

- Other development staff.

- Other staff, including the CEO, CFO, and program administrators.

- Key board members.

- Development committee.

Planning Meetings

It has been said that there are two kinds of people in the working world—those who attend meetings all day and those who take messages for those who are in meetings all day! While most people have more meetings in their day than they care to, a good plan cannot be done in a vacuum and will require meetings. Therefore, the organization needs to factor in the time spent in meeting into the planning process.

Like any good meeting, a carefully orchestrated planning meeting will keep people on task and, at the same time, build enthusiasm for the planning process. Remember what was stated earlier in this chapter: "The process is as important as the product."

How many meetings will it take? It depends, of course, on several factors, such as who is going to be involved, how much previous fundraising history must be analyzed, and whether this is the first plan the organization has done or if it will just involve updating a previous plan. Typically, there will be an initial meeting or perhaps a series of meetings with the entire development staff, and another with the development committee to analyze past development performance. If a consultant is being used, he or she should be involved in these initial meetings. Another meeting will be needed for setting goals and objectives, and this may involve the board and the development committee as well as the CEO and the CDO. Once the goals are established, staff will generally require several meetings to develop appropriate strategies and objectives for reaching these goals. Again, if a consultant is being used, they will most likely facilitate the goal setting meetings and will meet with the staff to help with strategies and objectives, or may develop the strategies and objectives themselves if the staff is limited or has little development experience. Once the plan is completed, it should be presented to the CEO in writing followed by a meeting between the CEO and the CDO to discuss the plan and any concerns the CEO may have. After the CEO has given his or her approval, it should be presented to the development committee, and then the development committee should present it to the board.

If a full-blown development audit has been done, the number of meetings spent analyzing the past performance can be eliminated, as this step will have already been completed. An audit, however, will generally take three months or so to complete, so that time will need to be factored into the planning process if the audit is pending.

Setting Goals and Objectives

Sometimes plans go astray because people set too many goals; do not understand the difference between goals, strategies, and objectives; or set goals but are not clear about how to establish objectives that will help them reach their goals. The first thing that must be made clear is the difference between goals and objectives. Goals are broad based, whereas objectives are more detailed. It might help to think of the plan as a road map. The development program has a starting point—the status of its current development program, which has been evaluated using the information in the preceding chapter. It also has a destination—where it wants its development program to be at the end of a year or two or three years. If a family were starting at a point on the map, perhaps New York, and it wanted to get to San Francisco, a quick look at the United States atlas would show the driver that the best way to do this would be to take Interstate Route 80. So, the family has a goal—to get to San Francisco via Interstate Route 80. This goal is part of the bigger vision of the family, perhaps to build a whole new life. Other goals of this vision may be to find a new job, to go back to school and prepare for a new career, to find housing in a rural setting, and to improve the family's health by living a healthier lifestyle. But, for the purposes of discussing goals, we will look at the goal of getting to San Francisco. The next step is to set reasonable objectives—stopping points along the way that can be measured, perhaps a first-day's drive to just outside Chicago, Illinois, a second-day's drive to Cheyenne, Wyoming, and a third-day's drive to the destination, San Francisco. Of course, the family must take several things into consideration—first, its strategy. Is it to be a leisurely sightseeing trip so they can see the country along the way, or is there

TIPS & TECHNIQUES

Some helpful tips for planning meetings (and meetings in general):

- Keep meetings brief—usually one hour is sufficient, except for the staff strategy meetings, which may go longer (however, even these meetings may be better broken into several meetings of one to one and a half hours each).

- Most people are at their best in the early morning, so this is a good time to conduct intense meetings such as the strategy developing session.

- Be sensitive to the time constraints of volunteers—they may be available only in the early morning, evening, etc.

- Always have an agenda, distribute it in advance, and stick to it.

- An e-mail reminder of the meeting works well for most people; however, some prefer a phone reminder. Know what is best for participants and use the method they prefer.

- The lead person in the planning process, usually the CDO, should lead the meetings, unless a consultant is being used, in which case he or she may facilitate the planning meetings.

- Always leave each meeting with a clear understanding of tasks to be accomplished before the next meeting and assignments for each task.

- Follow up with a brief written report of what was accomplished at the meeting, a reminder of the next meeting, and the tasks to be accomplished before that meeting.

a need to get to San Francisco as quickly as possible? Then the family needs to look at more tactical issues, such as how many people there are to take turns with the driving, weather conditions that could make driving difficult, mountainous roads, decisions about whether they want to get there as quickly as possible or sightsee along the way, and so on. They also need to consider what kind of resources will be needed—gas, safety equipment, food supplies, and the like, all of which can affect the final outcome of the trip. Then they need to develop more detailed action steps—what hotels they will stay in, how much they will cost, what stops they plan to make along the way and how much time each of these stops will require, who will be the principal driver and who will navigate the road maps, and so on.

The development office must determine broad-based goals, set reasonable objectives for each goal, and finally specific action steps for each objective, including a budget, timeline, and area of responsibility.

IN THE REAL WORLD

One development officer describes her development planning process as being similar to Mapquest. She says, "I find planning to be the map. Mapquest is probably a good example; we put in where we are and where we want to go—you need both of those elements for a development plan. You also need to know your strategy—do you want to take the fastest route, the most direct route, avoid interstate highways, and so on. Mapquest then tells us the route to follow, the timetable, and the distance. In development, we need to know the strategy, step by step; how long each step takes; and what we need to do at each turn. Mapquest, however, does make mistakes—sending us down one-way streets, into construction, and so on. Development plans are not perfect because internal and external environmental issues happen—we need to be able to make U-turns or back up, maybe even get a smaller car to zip through traffic. Likewise, flexibility plays a major role in the development plan."

Examples of broad-based goals for a development plan might be to raise awareness of the organization, to get the board more involved in fundraising, to increase the organization's major-gift program, or to decrease its reliance on grant funding. These are ultimate destinations, broad-based goals that will guide the objectives and, ultimately, the action steps of the plan. In most cases, three to seven broad-based goals are sufficient for a development plan. Some organizations set too many goals because they confuse goals with the more detailed objectives. This will result in lack of direction and confusion about which goals should be high priority. The goals must be visionary but attainable.

Strategy

Strategy is more about the how and why we do what we do. For example, for the goal of getting more board involvement, some strategies might include educating the board about philanthropy, developing a new board, and building better relationships between the board and staff. Why does the board need education? A board that does not understand philanthropy, development, and fundraising will certainly be reluctant to become involved and may even oppose the whole development plan. So a strategy of board education about philanthropy will help them feel more at ease about fundraising and will help them see how important it is for those outside the organization to see their support of the development program. Then, objectives can be put into place to make this happen. Objectives for this strategy might include things like engaging a consultant to do a board retreat or a board workshop, and action steps to support this would be to hire the consultant, plan the agenda, establish the time and location, and so on.

Objectives

Objectives are the more detailed areas of the plan. Like the family heading to San Francisco, they must have some measurable objectives. Some things they might consider as benchmarks are how many miles can be driven each day, historic sites they want to visit, and allowing time to buy groceries and do laundry. What

TIPS & TECHNIQUES

Objectives must be SMART objectives:

- **S**pecific

- **M**easurable

- **A**ction oriented

- **R**ealistic (but visionary)

- **T**ime defined

are the alternatives if we don't make it to Chicago the first night because we had bad weather or someone got sick? Development plan objectives cannot be set in stone any more than a trip across the country. The plan must allow for contingencies such as loss of a key development staff member, a major national or local crisis that might affect the organization's fundraising, and so on.

Unlike the broad-based goals, objectives will be more specific. For example, if one of the goals was to raise awareness of the organization, objectives might include:

- Establish a Web site that includes online giving opportunities by December 2007.

- Develop and distribute a press kit to local media annually by the end of January 2008.

- Hold one donor cultivation event each month during 2008.

Each of these objectives meets the above criteria. They are specific, defining exactly what the organization is going to do to raise awareness. They are measurable—the organization can determine if the Web site has been completed by December, can report on the progress of the annual distribution of press kits, and can easi-ly track the progress of monthly cultivation events. Likewise, the objectives are action oriented; each one of them requires specific actions to implement. For most organizations, these seem like reasonable objectives, but each organization must assess how doable the action steps for each objective are for their organization before including them in the plan. If, for example, the organization whose objective is to hold monthly donor cultivation events has 12 board mem-bers and each one agrees to host one cultivation event a year, holding monthly cultivation events seems attainable. But if the board has no interest in this process, and the staff feel they need board support to hold cultivation events, this may not be a reasonable objective. Similarly, if it is now October 2007, having a new Web site designed by December may not be realistic. It is important to remember that while objectives should be realistic, they should also involve a stretch on the part of staff and board. Don't set goals and objectives that are too easy to attain, or they will not be worth working toward. Each of the steps above has a defi-nite timeline. Again, these timelines are not set in stone, but the organization should establish timelines that are reasonable to accomplish and can be used as a benchmark to measure the plan's progress.

Assigning Timelines, Budgets, and Areas of Responsibility

Perhaps the biggest mistake made in the planning process is setting goals, strate-gies, and objectives, but not taking the final step—assigning specific action steps that have budgets, timelines, and areas of responsibility assigned to them. Many or-ganizations think that if they establish the goals, strategies, and objectives, they've done a plan. This false thinking has caused many organizations to wonder later why their plan has been sitting on a shelf, instead of being a vital, working document.

For example, going back to the hypothetical objectives listed above, let's look at some action steps that would help reach these objectives, resulting in a goal's being reached. If the organization is to design a new Web site, some specific actions might include things like:

- Evaluate the current Web site to see which items need to be changed and which can be kept as is.
  - Responsibility—director of development and PR director
  - Budget—N/A
  - Timeline—June 30, 2007

- Prepare and distribute a request for proposal (RFP) for Web site designers.
  - Responsibility—PR director
  - Budget—$5,000
  - Timeline—July 31, 2007

- Interview designers.
  - Responsibility—PR director and director of development
  - Budget—N/A
  - Timeline—August 31, 2007

- Select a Web site designer
  - Responsibility—PR director
  - Budget—N/A
  - Timeline—September 30, 2007

- Complete design.
  - Responsibility—Web site designer/PR director/director of development
  - Budget—see above
  - Timeline—December 31, 2007

Similarly, for the objective of preparing and distributing media kits, some action steps might include:

- Determine what materials the media packet should contain.

  - Responsibility—director of development/PR director
  - Budget—N/A
  - Timeline—November 30, 2007

- Prepare the media packet.

  - Responsibility—development assistant
  - Budget—$500
  - Timeline—December 31, 2007

- Develop a list of media contacts.

  - Responsibility—PR assistant
  - Budget—N/A
  - Timeline—December 31, 2007

- Distribute the media kits in person to each contact.

  - Responsibility—director of development
  - Budget—$100
  - Timeline—January 31, 2007

For the final objective, assuming the board has agreed that this is a realistic objective, some action steps might include:

- Prepare a schedule for board members hosting events.

  - Responsibility—director of development/board
  - Budget—N/A
  - Timeline—September 30, 2007

- Prepare invitation list.

  o Responsibility—individual board members and director of development

  o Budget—N/A

  o Timeline—monthly beginning October 1, 2007

- Secure location and make plans for refreshments.

  o Responsibility—development assistant

  o Budget—N/A

  o Timeline—monthly beginning November 1, 2007

- Prepare agenda.

  o Responsibility—director of development

  o Budget—N/A

  o Timeline—October 31, 2007

- Send invitation and accept RSVPs.

  o Responsibility—development assistant

  o Budget—$50 each event

  o Timeline—monthly beginning January 1, 2008

- Call to remind attendees of event.

  o Responsibility—development assistant

  o Budget—N/A

  o Timeline—monthly beginning February 1, 2008

- Hold event.

  o Responsibility—director of development/executive director/individual board members

  o Budget—$200 each event

  o Timeline—monthly beginning February 15, 2008

- Hold debriefing session and plan follow-up.
  - Responsibility—director of development/executive director/individual board members
  - Budget—N/A
  - Timeline—monthly beginning March 1, 2008

Summary

The first step in preparing the development plan is to decide who needs to be involved. Typically, the CDO heads up a planning committee. Other people who should be involved in the planning process include:

- CEO
- CFO
- Program department administrators
- All development staff
- Key board members
- Development committee members

Some of these people may not be on the planning committee but should be consulted for their particular expertise and the value of their involvement.

Meetings should be brief but productive. The evaluation and task assignment meetings with the development staff (assuming there is a staff) will be more detailed.

Goals should be set with input from the CEO, the CFO, and the board. The development committee will have a larger role in the planning process, especially for smaller organizations. If there is no development staff, it is usually the development committee that does the plan. If there is a staff, and the organization has a fairly sophisticated fundraising program, often the development committee members are more involved in implementing the plan than in developing it. The development committee should present the plan to the board to get their buy-in.

Goals and objectives must be set for each area. Objectives are more specific than goals and should always be SMART:

- Specific

- Measurable

- Action oriented

- Realistic (but visionary)

- Time defined

Once the goals and objectives have been established, the staff is responsible for developing action steps for each objective that include timelines, budgets, and areas of responsibility.

EXHIBIT 4.1

XYZ Organization Development Plan

Goal	Strategy	Objective	Action Step	Responsible Person or Team	Budget Positive or (Negative)	Time to Be Completed

EXHIBIT 4.2

XYZ Organization
Development Planning Schedule

Development Planning Step	Who Needs to Be Involved	Timeline for Completion	Resources Needed
Assess Past Development Performance			
Review Mission			
Review or Determine Vision			
Complete SWOT Analysis			
Establish Goals			
Determine Strategy			
Set Objectives			
Develop Action Steps			
Assign Areas of Responsibility			
Assign Budget (income and expenses)			
Establish Timelines			
Establish Evaluation Process			
Produce Written Planning Document			
Produce Written Planning Document			

continued on the next page

Development Planning Step	Who Needs to Be Involved	Timeline for Completion	Resources Needed
Present Plan to Management			
Present Plan to Board			
Evaluate Plan			
Prepare for Next Planning Cycle			

CHAPTER 5

The Product

"No farmer ever plowed a field by turning it over in his (or her) mind."
George E. Woodbury

After reading this chapter, you will be able to:

- List the various components of the development plan.
- Plan a format for the written planning document.
- Develop a process to have the plan approved.

A plan is not a plan until it is in writing. The development officer cannot hold the plan in his or her mind; it must be written, approved, and evaluated if it is to be implemented successfully. At the end of this chapter, the reader will find some sample formats for presenting the plan in written form (Exhibit 5.1). But first, let us examine the components of the plan. A typical development plan includes goals, objectives, strategies, and action steps in the following areas:

- Infrastructure
- Donor relations
- Communications

- Fundraising activities

- Fundraising methods

Infrastructure includes the following areas:

- Technology

- Staffing

- Board involvement in fundraising

- Volunteer involvement in fundraising

Technology

Technology is an important part of the development plan and includes the availability and use of a donor software system, adequate hardware, and other software systems to assist the development office in carrying out the development functions. During the assessment phase of the planning process, the organization should look at its current systems and determine if there are any goals or objectives relating to technology that need to be addressed.

Many smaller organizations and those who are new to fundraising may think they can save money by not using a donor software system, trying to track donor information and contributions using generic products such as Access, Excel, or ACT instead. While these are all good programs for the purposes for which they were intended, they will not serve the development office that is trying to move its program to a higher level of sophistication. The development office needs to have a software program that will allow the tracking of donor history; pledges and pledge payments; personal information about the donor such as birthdates and names of children; and notes on contacts with the donor. There are a number of programs available, ranging in costs from free to $50,000 or more. Each development office should assess its needs and select a software system that best meets those needs and is within the department's budget for technology support.

A good donor software tracking system will allow the organization to:

- Merge personalized letters and print personalized envelopes for donors and prospects.

- Record multi-payment pledges and generate pledge reminders.

- Track donor history, including matching gifts, restricted gifts, as well as unrestricted gifts.

- Record donor preferences such as "Do not mail," "Do not call," and so on.

- Report increases in giving for individuals and groups of donors.

- Generate acknowledgment letters and gift receipts.

- Produce reports showing results of special event fundraising, differentiating between contributions, sponsorships, and attendance fees.

- Generate cash flow reports based on projected pledge payment schedules.

- Produce lists of LYBUNTs and SYBUNTs (donors who gave in previous years but have not given currently—Last Year But Unfortunately Not This and Some Years But Unfortunately Not This).

- Generate management reports for board and executive management showing the results of various fundraising methods and programs.

- Additional functions needed by the organization such as tracking membership programs, grant funding, and so on.

If there is a software system in place, it should be evaluated periodically to determine if it is still performing to a standard required by the development office. Many times, organizations make an investment in a good software system but do not fully utilize the software to the extent they could. Or the person who has been trained to use the software has left the organization, leaving no one trained to use the software to its full capacity. All of these things should be assessed and objectives established for technology upgrades, training, or ongoing support within the overall infrastructure goal.

Technology needs in the form of hardware and software should also be a part of the development plan. It is important to be able to communicate with funders and donors in a timely and efficient manner. Computer upgrades, state-of-the-art wireless technology, smart phones, Internet capability, and a good scheduling program such as Outlook are all essentials for the development office. If updates are needed in any of these areas, they should be included in the development plan.

Staffing

Another important aspect of the infrastructure for development is staffing. The organization should consider not only whether it has adequate staffing in the development office, but also whether it has the *right* staff and the right staffing organizational structure, and whether it provides staff with the tools needed to perform their development functions.

Many organizations have a limited development staff and yet expect the staff to do special events, grant writing, major gifts, and, oh yes, then there is the development office budget, the public relations functions, the development plan, and so on. How much staff is enough to run a solid development program? The answer will depend on what roles this person or persons are expected to fill. Is there a separate public relations department that will handle that function? Do program people write their own grants or at least identify potential funding sources? How many events does the organization run? How many major donors is the development officer expected to visit each month? What are the financial and other goals of the development program? If the internal assessment reveals that the staff is so overburdened with grants or events that they do not have time to visit with major donors, then the plan should outline alternatives to reach the objectives stated. Perhaps special events or grant research and writing can be outsourced to a contracted consultant. Perhaps some events should be eliminated. Possibly, the major donor calls need to be limited to a smaller number, or more board and volunteer involvement can replace staff time devoted to major-gift calls. Or perhaps it is time to add more staff. If this is the case, the plan should outline what the role of these additional staff people will be and list a timeline and budget for hiring the new staff.

Another aspect of staffing that is important is whether the organization has the right people doing the right jobs within development. It is sometimes difficult to find someone who has the skills to write well, conduct research, do planning and budgeting, and at the same time be considered a "people person" who can successfully solicit major donors, relate well to the corporate funders, and develop life-long relationships with other constituents of the organization. A strong development program will build on the skills of the staff and at the same time stretch the staff to grow and assume new and more challenging roles. The plan may call for a reorganization of the current development office in order to ensure maximum efficiency and utilization of the appropriate skills and talents of each staff member.

It is important to remember that the development office should coordinate all fundraising activities of the organization, and the department must be structured in such a way that this coordination is possible. This includes the assurance that the development office reports directly to the chief executive officer (CEO) of the organization and that it is on the same level with other major departments of the organization such as program, finance, and marketing/public relations.

A typical organizational chart for a large and a small development office is found at the end of this chapter (Exhibits 5.2 and 5.3). Of course, in a very small office, there may be just *one* person to do all the development functions. This may

During the planning process, one organization realized it had enough staff people; they just were not assigned to the right tasks to match their skills and interests. For example, the administrative assistant had a great rapport with the alumni, was an alum herself, and was therefore promoted to the position of alumni director, while some of her administrative duties were handed off to the secretary to the vice president and the database coordinator. The receptionist, it was determined, had a real knack for research and had great computer skills, so she was assigned the additional duty of conducting research for the small development office. One of the public relations people was good at planning events, so she was transferred into the development office to work on special events. Additional training was planned for those staff people who assumed new duties and a flex-time schedule was worked out to improve productivity. Without hiring any additional staff, this office was able to increase its contributions by 50 percent and staff morale increased greatly.

result in the plan's being narrower in scope, and it may be more challenging to implement the development plan, but it will still be important for the organization to have a development plan.

Board Involvement in Fundraising

The internal assessment may reveal weaknesses in the board's involvement in the fundraising activities of the organization. This is usually the result of improper board recruitment methods leading to board members thinking that they will not be required to do fundraising and perhaps not even to contribute to the organization themselves. In cases where the board is not as involved in fundraising as they could or should be, the plan will certainly need to include some strategies to improve board giving and/or board involvement in the development plan. For this reason, it is wise to reiterate what was said in Chapter 4: The board must be involved with setting goals for the development plan if they are expected to help implement the plan.

Every development plan should include an annual board appeal. This appeal should be conducted at the beginning of the fiscal year so that when the organization launches its community-wide appeal, it can say that it has 100 percent participation of the board in its fundraising effort. This will be an important benchmark to track success. Particularly for organizations that plan to apply for foundation funding, the question will surely be asked by potential funders, "What percentage of your board contribute financially to the organization?"

Some organizations make the mistake of announcing at a board meeting that the board is expected to give and then distribute pledge cards, asking them to complete them and turn them in before they leave that meeting. This often turns off board members, especially if they were not expecting to be asked for a contribution. It is critical to have a position description in place that clearly outlines financial expectations of the board and that these position descriptions are reviewed with potential board members *before* they agree to serve on the board, not given out at orientation after they have already been elected to the board. If the board members do not have an adequate position description or the position description is not being used properly, this should be one of the objectives in the plan to support the goal of increased board involvement in fundraising.

The board appeal should be a formal appeal, structured like any other constituency appeal. Board members should be evaluated for a potential ask amount, and a team of volunteers from the board should agree to serve on a board appeal committee to invite participation from the rest of the board. A presentation on the importance of board giving can be made by a board member, a staff person, or an outside consultant. It is generally better for this presentation to come from a peer board member or an outside consultant, perhaps even a board member from another nonprofit that has strong board participation. Sometimes a staff member is put in the difficult position of being the person telling the board they must give. However, the staff can and should support the board appeal committee in its approach to the board members, particularly with providing research on past giving patterns of the board members. Like any other major donor, board members should be invited individually and personally to make their commitment, giving it the importance it deserves. A formal board appeal is often another objective in the plan to support the goal of increased board involvement.

Another objective to support increased board involvement in fundraising might include the formation or strengthening of a development committee on the board. The development committee should consist of both board and non–board members, thereby expanding the technical skills and reach of the committee. If the organization does not already have a development committee, objectives might include developing one. Some action steps needed to reach this objective could include developing a title and position description for the committee, identifying potential members of the committee, and recruiting the committee members. If the organization already has a committee in place, it may, depending on the internal assessment findings, need to recruit additional members, refine the role of the committee, or ensure that the committee members have the training and skills they need to be effective members of the development team. If the committee is already a strong one, the plan might address issues such as the development committee's further involvement in identifying, cultivating, and soliciting potential donors or expanding its role in training and encouraging the board of directors in its fundraising efforts.

Once the board has made its own commitment to contribute to the organization and accepts its fundraising role, the plan may need to address issues such as helping the board feel more comfortable in a fundraising role. Board training can be an objective of the plan. Ongoing board education in the form of a presentation at each board meeting by the development office is one step toward ensuring this objective. Another would be to conduct a board retreat or a special board training program relating to fundraising. This will be especially helpful if the organization is about to enter a capital campaign or undertake a major fundraising effort. Special training in planned giving, e-philanthropy, or other specialized areas might also benefit board members and make them feel more comfortable with their fundraising role. A brainstorming session to help board members identify potential donors for the organization may also be helpful; a form to assist the development office in this process is included at the end of this chapter (Exhibit 5.4).

TIPS & TECHNIQUES

Some key factors to measure the board's involvement in fundraising include:

- The board should demonstrate 100 percent commitment to the annual fund.

- If the organization is in a capital campaign, the board's 100 percent commitment should be obtained during the leadership phase and before the public phase of the campaign is launched.

- Board members should individually strive to make a planned gift to the organization.

- Board members should be willing to identify potential donors for the organization.

- Board members should be willing to host cultivation events for donors either in their homes or at the organization's facility.

- Board members should be willing to solicit prospective donors or to open doors for the organization to solicit them.

- There should be a development committee consisting of board and non–board members.

Volunteer Fundraisers

In addition to members of the development committee, there are other volunteer roles that can enhance and improve the organization's fundraising program. During the assessment phase of the plan, the organization should look at the ways it uses volunteers in its fundraising program, the number of volunteers utilized, the skills and talents of these volunteers, and the training and recognition provided for volunteers.

Often, volunteers are brought only into the fringes of development, working on special events. If the organization does not use volunteers in its other fundraising efforts, it may be losing out on the valuable expertise and numerous contacts these volunteers may have. For example, an organization can benefit from a planned giving committee or council made up of community volunteers with specialized skills in planned giving—an estate planner, an estate attorney, a financial planner, an accountant, an insurance broker, a bank trust officer. These volunteers can help the organization develop its planned giving program, conduct planned giving seminars, and promote the organization's planned giving program to their clients.

Volunteers can also be helpful in running a corporate appeal. Often, organizations struggle with how to approach local corporations and businesses and attempt to run their corporate/business appeal using direct mail or staff members to solicit corporate leaders. A peer-to-peer approach is always more successful, so the plan should include an annual appeal to local businesses that involves volunteers making the ask. *Recruiting and Training Fundraising Volunteers* includes a section devoted to organizing a corporate appeal using volunteers.

If the organization has not been involving volunteers in its fundraising efforts, it should look at developing some objectives toward this end in the development plan—establishing a development committee, a major-gifts committee, a planned giving council, a business appeal committee, and the like. The plan should also contain the actions steps necessary to complete these objectives.

TIPS & TECHNIQUES

Some of the ways to involve volunteers in the fundraising program include:

- Capital campaign cabinet
- Capital campaign committees
- Planned giving council
- Development committee
- Corporate and business appeal
- Telephone appeal
- Mail appeal
- Special events

Volunteers will be particularly critical if the organization is contemplating a capital campaign in the future. Involving volunteers in the development program on an annual basis makes it much easier to recruit volunteers for the capital campaign.

Involving more volunteers can be an objective in itself or can be included with the action steps for each campaign or appeal listed in the plan.

Donor Relations

The next component of the plan is donor relations. During the assessment phase of the plan, the organization should look at its current strategies for identifying, cultivating, and providing good stewardship for its donors. Any areas of weakness in these areas need to be addressed in the plan.

TIPS & TECHNIQUES

Some important steps in developing a volunteer committee include:

- Prepare an organizational chart for the structure of the committee.

- Prepare a plan for each committee that includes the timeline for its activities (i.e., is it an ongoing committee, such as the development committee, or a short-term project like an event or a capital campaign?).

- Prepare a position description for each volunteer position in the organizational chart.

- Develop a list of the skills needed by each volunteer.

- Develop a list of potential volunteers who meet these criteria.

- Prepare a volunteer recruitment packet.

- Have the right person ask the volunteer to join the committee.

- Recruit the volunteers.

- Plan a volunteer orientation.

- Provide ongoing education for the volunteers.

- Recognize the volunteer for their efforts.

Identifying Donors

Some organizations are fortunate to have a "built-in" audience for their fundraising activities—for example, alumni of a school, grateful patients of a hospital, residents of a nonprofit retirement community, and the like. Others need to spend more time identifying potential donors for their organization. Even those who have a list of likely donors must spend time researching these donors for their ability linkage and interest in the organization's programs. Therefore, a solid research component is an important part of the development plan.

Identifying Prospective Donors

For organizations that do not have a logical pool of constituents from which to draw, the first step may be finding people who have an interest in the organization. Rosso's concentric circles of involvement tells us that best place to start is with the inside circle, the "family" of the organization—board members, staff, users of the organization's services. Then, move out to the outer circles of involvement— vendors, parents, alumni, and the like—before reaching the community at large. Depending on the organization's size and scope of activities, there may be smaller or greater numbers of people within these various circles. If the organization has not researched those closest to it, this should be an objective within the goal of improving donor relations. The organization should first know its own trustees and employees. A simple board of directors' fact sheet can be a good place to start, and a sample is found at the end of this chapter (Exhibit 5.5).

Once the organization has identified all the people closest to it, there may be a need for a formal research program to identify a broader range of potential donors. For some organizations, a direct mail acquisition is the first place to start identifying individual donors. Once they have obtained what tend to be smaller donations from the first direct mail appeal, they can build a donor base and then, using an electronic screening research firm, determine if there are potential major donors within this donor pool. If the organization has not yet reached the point of having a large database of potential donors, it may want to utilize more informal researching methods. A staff member or volunteer can search the Internet using Google or another search engine. It is amazing how much public information is available about constituents. For corporations, annual reports are available and many list their giving policies either in their annual report or online. A series of screening sessions with the board and/or development committee can also be helpful in refining the information on file about potential donors or identifying new people to add to the list. Using the Potential Donors for Our Organization form at the end of this chapter (Exhibit 5.4) can be a helpful way to develop a prospect list.

Foundation research is perhaps the easiest of all the types of research done by many organizations, since foundations are required by law to report their assets and disbursements on their 990 forms. Most of this information is also available through a number of electronic search platforms including the Foundation Center, the Big Online Database, and Grant Station, which is the most comprehensive of the tools listed, Covering Foundation, Corporate and Government Funding Sources.

 TIPS & TECHNIQUES

Research methods include:

- Electronic research firms that can identify the wealth factors and interest of your prospective donors.

- Internet searches on Google or other search engines for individuals, corporations, and foundations.

- Foundation research at libraries, through directories, or online at www.GrantStation.com, www.bigdatabase.com, or www.foundationcenter.org.

- Informal research such as clipping newspaper articles about donors and prospective donors.

- Annual reports of other nonprofits, especially those with a similar mission to the organization doing the research.

- Screening sessions with board, development committee, or a special donor identification committee.

For the development plan, each organization must determine what type of research it needs and then develop strategies for doing the research. For example, will it utilize an outside research firm, hire a researcher, assign this duty to a current staff member, or ask a volunteer to take on this task? Regardless of how it decides to proceed, it will be critical that sensitive information about donors and prospective donors is handled confidentially and ethically.

Stewardship

Providing good stewardship to donors is a critical part of the donor relations program. A survey conducted several years ago by Carnegie Mellon University indicated that the one thing donors want above anything else they expect from the organizations to which they contributed is a report of how their money was used. The development plan must include strategies for improving donor relations. Following the Donor Bill of Rights found at the end of this chapter (Exhibit 5.6) is an excellent guideline for providing good stewardship. Some things that might be covered in the plan, if they are found lacking during the assessment phase, are reviewing donor acknowledgment letters to ensure that they not only meet the IRS requirements, but that they show donors how their money was used; to develop an appropriate donor recognition program; to establish a donor reporting system for restricted donations; and to educate the staff, board and volunteers on the Donor Bill of Rights.

Donor acknowledgments must be done on a timely basis; within 24 to 48 hours of receipt of a gift is recommended. And the acknowledgments must be accurate. The donor database should be used to generate all receipts, acknowledgment letters, and other donor correspondence to ensure accuracy. The letters should be warm and personal, recognizing the donor's gift amount and telling the donor how his or her money was used. All acknowledgments should be personally signed by a staff member, board member, or volunteer who solicited the gift. If the organization needs to beef up its acknowledgment processes, this should be part of the development plan.

The Rule of Seven

Donors should be thanked seven times before they are asked for the next gift. Some ways to thank donors include:

- A handwritten note from the person who solicited the gift.
- An official receipt signed by the director of development.
- A personal letter signed by the CEO or board chair.
- Listing in the newsletter (providing, of course, that the donor did not request that he or she remain anonymous).
- Listing in the annual report (again, if the donor did not request that he or she remain anonymous).
- A phone call from a board member, recipient of services, or volunteer.
- A formal donor recognition event.
- The donor's name on a plaque, brick walkway, or other formal recognition vehicle (again, only if he or she does not wish to remain anonymous).
- Any other creative way the organization has for thanking its donors.

Cultivation Techniques

Donor cultivation is another step in the process of donor relations. If the organization is found to have weaknesses in this area, the plan might address some strategies to cultivate existing donors and prospective donors. Many organizations plan regular cultivation events, at which no donations are solicited, but information is given and received. These cultivation events can be extremely valuable

TIPS & TECHNIQUES

Some cultivation activities include:

- Small informal luncheons with individual donors and the CEO of the organization and/or a key board member.

- Open house–type events where small or large groups tour the facility and take part in a prepared presentation about the organization and its programs.

- Cocktail parties or dinner parties in the home of a board member or other volunteer.

- Business leader breakfasts with a brief presentation about the organization.

- Mobile tours, where the prospective donors are driven in a van or bus around the organization's campus.

in preparing for a major–gift program or capital campaign, through which donors will be asked later for significant gifts.

Communications

In addition to donor communications, the organization needs to focus on its communications to the public. Some organizations have a separate public relations department that develops its own communications plan. If this is the case, it is important for the development office to work closely with the communications people to ensure that communications with the public reflect a solid fundraising slant. For example, the development office might be responsible for a page or several pages of the organization's Web site that focus on fund development. Or the development office might write a column for the newsletter focusing on donor issues. If the development office is also responsible for the entire communications and public relations program, the development plan should have specific goals for this area. Typically, an organization's communications media include:

- Case for support.

- Brochures and other written fundraising materials.

- Program brochures.

- Web site.

- Annual report.

- Media (press) kits.

- Media (press) releases.

The first place to start is to develop a compelling case for support for the organization's fundraising programs. The case for the organization is larger in scope than the case statement for an individual project, say a capital campaign; however, many organizations tend to think they only need a case statement for their individual fundraising programs. In actuality, they should begin with the overall organizational case and then develop individual case statements from this case. Timothy L. Seiler, in *Developing Your Case for Support*, provides the Association of Fundraising Professionals (AFP) definition of a case and a case statement (from the AFP *Fundraising Dictionary*) to help the reader distinguish between the two:

Case—the reasons why an organization both needs and merits philanthropic support, usually by outlining the organization's programs, current needs, and plans.

Case statement—a presentation that sets forth the case.

Seiler's book outlines step by step how to develop a case and the various case statements that will be presented. For organizations that have overlooked this important first step in fundraising, Seiler's book is an excellent resource to get them started.

Once the case has been developed and case statements for each various program and each constituency can be planned, the next step is developing written and other materials from the case, such as brochures, Web pages, PowerPoint presentations, speeches, grant proposals, and the like. If the organization has a case, its plan might include ways to translate that case for its various constituencies. It is important to do the case first so all fundraising and program materials have the organization's unique brand, logo, and theme. Part of the development plan should include a review and updating of materials that may not reflect this image. There should be a whole package of development materials planned, including brochures, letterhead and envelopes, response envelopes, fact sheets, pledge cards, and other useful development tools—all reflecting the same uniform theme and image.

Web Site

Many organizations are using their Web sites to promote philanthropy and fundraising. In the assessment phase, the organization's Web site should be evaluated to see if it is user friendly, promotes philanthropy, and provides potential donors with an expeditious way to contribute to the organization. A planned giving page is also a helpful educational tool for prospective donors and one that can result in large gifts to the organization, providing there is a way to gather information on who visits the site and follow-up to potential donors is part of the plan. Even if there is a separate department that is responsible for the Web site, the development office should have major input into the fundraising sections of the Web site. If the organization's Web site needs upgrading, the development plan should address this issue.

Annual Report

If an organization has limited funds to spend for communications pieces, the annual report is a great tool to get the most bang for the buck. An annual report should list all donors to the organization, tell stories and show pictures about

One organization that was new to fundraising had never done an annual report. When it hired its first director of development, he suggested an annual report. Some board members had several concerns: (1) an annual report would be costly to print and mail to their 10,000-name mailing list; (2) they had just solicited donors in their direct mail program and did not want to have the report misconstrued as another solicitation piece, and (3) they had recently changed accounting methods and were afraid the anticipated deficit they reported might have a negative affect on potential donors. The development director handled these objections carefully. First, he was able to obtain a gift-in-kind from a local printer and design house, so the only expense would be the mailing costs. Also, a response envelope would be included in the annual report, but no direct ask for money, thereby relieving the fears of a double ask, while still opening the door to potential contributions that could cover the cost of the mailing. Furthermore, the board finance chair prepared a written statement addressing the concern about the deficit budget, which would be given to every employee and kept by their phone in the event that they received phone calls about the financial report.

The report was produced, showing all the progress the organization had made in its programs during the past year, and was mailed to almost 10,000 people. The result—enough money came in through the response envelopes, many from people who had already made a gift to the annual fund, to more than cover the costs of the annual report. Three phone calls were received after the report was delivered—all from donors regarding the donor listing—one whose name was spelled wrong, one who had given after the listed June 30 cutoff date but wondered why her gift was not listed, and the third from a donor who had actually given to another organization but thought she had given to this one. Lesson learned—what donors are really interested in is how their money was used, and in getting proper recognition for their gifts!

people that have benefited from its programs, and present its financial report. This piece will serve as an excellent fundraising tool, so even if there is a communications or public relations department that does the annual report, the development office should have a great deal of input into the report. Often, the development office is asked only to provide the list of donors, but they can also contribute stories about donors, planned giving articles, and other information that can make the annual report an excellent fundraising tool. If the organization does not currently produce an annual report, this could be an excellent objective for the development plan.

Media (Press) Kits and Media (Press) Releases

The development office needs to ensure that the organization has good media relations. A great tool that can help with this area is a media kit, which can be delivered to reporters, newscasters, and radio show hosts. Again, if there is a communications/public relations office, it may handle this task, but the development office should have input into this process. Often, the development people are the front-line communicators for their organization and should strive to develop good relationships with the media. If there is no public relations office, the task of preparing media kits and media releases will probably fall to the development office. The plan should, in either case, address the issue of media relations, either by providing input into the public relations plan or developing objectives for the development plan that address this issue.

Fundraising Activities and Constituencies

Fundraising activities are generally divided into three broad categories—annual fund, capital campaigns, and planned giving. The annual fund and capital campaigns usually involve strategies to reach several constituencies—individuals, corporations, and foundations—whereas planned giving generally focuses strictly on individual giving. Organizations are sometimes approached as a group, or they may request a written proposal. The annual fund should be included in every development plan, since it is the bedrock of the development program. Annual giving strategies will include several different fundraising methods such as grant research and proposal writing, special events, direct mail, telephone solicitation appeal, corporate and business appeal, and individual solicitation.

Some organizations may be preparing for a capital campaign, in which case there will be a detailed capital campaign plan, but highlights of this plan should be included in the overall development plan, particularly where the campaign may overlap with activities of the annual fundraising program. If the organization is preparing for a future capital campaign, there may be several steps included in the development plan in anticipation of a future campaign. These strategies could include recruiting a capital campaign steering committee, board development, increased research and cultivation activities, or conducting a planning study.

Most organizations today are also in some phase of a planned giving program—just beginning a program, expanding their current efforts, or maintaining an existing program—so the plan should take this into account as well. Strategies for implementing the planned giving program might include developing planned giving seminars, adding a planned giving page to the Web site and/or the newsletter, requesting planned gifts on response envelopes, and/or developing a planned giving society.

Fundraising Methods

The various fundraising activities outlined above will utilize a number of fundraising methods that can serve as actions steps to support overall goals, objectives, and strategies of the development plan. For example, in the annual fund, most organizations use a number of methods including:

- Grants
- Special events
- Direct mail

- Web-based fundraising

- Telephone fundraising

- Corporate appeal, using personal solicitation

- Individual appeal for major gifts, also using personal solicitation

In a capital campaign, most of the lead gifts are a result of personal solicitations, along with government and foundation grants, which require a written proposal, sometimes followed by a personal presentation to the funder. Planned giving is almost always done through personal solicitation. The action steps to support goals of increasing or developing various programs in the plan might include things like establishing a Web-based giving program through PayPal or a similar vendor, recruiting a team of volunteers to serve on the corporate appeal, training the board to conduct solicitations, planning a series of cultivation events, engaging a telephone fundraising firm or recruiting volunteers to do a phonathon, planning (or eliminating) a special event, conducting research into potential foundation funders, and so on. It is critical that the plan include a variety of fundraising methods and techniques so the organization is not dependent on a single source of funding.

Format

The plan will generally contain a narrative explaining the goals and the strategies that will be used to achieve these goals. The plan may also contain a report of the findings of the internal assessment or development audit that led to the decision to include certain goals, objectives, and strategies. The written document should include the process for developing the plan and a section on how the plan will be evaluated and adjusted if necessary. Most plans are done in a table format, so they are easy to follow. The plan should also break down each action step by timeline, budgets, and areas of responsibility, so the organization can get an overview of each of these areas separately from the overall document. The timeline is a good benchmark for measuring the plan and can be used at staff meetings to assess progress. Some sample sections of plans are included at the end of this chapter (Exhibit 5.1) to help readers determine the format that works best for them.

Approval

The finished product must be approved by all the people and groups that will be involved with implementing the plan. It is wise to get approval on the goals from the CEO and/or board before spending a lot of time developing the strategies and action steps that will be used to achieve the goals. Once the board has approved the goals, objectives, and strategies, the development office will fill in the detailed action steps to achieve the goals. In most organizations, the development budget for the plan must be approved, but the organization's leadership may not be as concerned about some of the day-to-day details. Timelines, however, may be important, as they affect other programs and departments of the organization. For example, a new program may be planned only if government or foundation funding can be secured to fund the program. A capital campaign may need to be delayed if the development office needs more time to research and cultivate major donors or the board needs to be strengthened. The areas of responsibility that fall outside of the development office also need approval. If the board, for example, is expected to participate in the implementation of fundraising activities, they must approve the final plan before it is considered completed.

Summary

A typical development plan includes goals and objectives in the following areas:

- Infrastructure

- Donor relations

- Communications

- Fundraising activities and constituencies

- Fundraising methods

Infrastructure issues that are typically addressed in the plan include technology needs, staffing, board involvement in fundraising, and volunteer involvement in fundraising. The organization should assess its strengths and weaknesses in each of these areas and then develop objectives that meet the needs of the organization to enhance or expand these areas of its infrastructure. Without a solid base in place, it will be difficult for the organization to increase its fundraising results.

Good donor relations are also critical to success, and the plan should address areas of research, cultivation, and stewardship of the organization's donors and prospective donors. Following the Donor Bill of Rights will help ensure that all donors are treated with respect and consideration.

Various forms of research can be done by the development office, ranging from informal meetings with prospective donors to Internet, electronic screening of donors and prospects, and screening sessions with the board and volunteers. These should be part of the development plan. Many organizations include in their plan the use of various forms of cultivation strategies, including open house events, individual luncheons, business leaders' breakfasts, and dinners or cocktail parties in the homes of board members or volunteers.

Communications with the pubic are important to help create awareness of the organization before asking for contributions. Preparing a compelling case for support should be the first step in developing a package of fundraising material that includes brochures, fact sheets, pledge cards, response envelopes, letterhead and envelopes, grant proposals, speeches, and PowerPoint presentations—all with a uniform theme and look. Media relations are also important and should be part of the plan. The organization's Web site should also be used as a tool to educate people about philanthropy and about the organization, and can be used to solicit donations as well. If there is a public relations department within the organization, it is most likely primarily responsible for these activities, but the development office should have input into the fundraising aspects of these materials. If there is no public relations department, the development office is usually responsible for communications.

Several areas of fundraising activities are usually addressed in the plan—the annual fund, capital campaigns, and planned giving. All organizations should do an annual fund, some may be preparing for a capital campaign, and most are at least in the planning stages for, if not already involved in, a planned giving program. All of these areas should be addressed in the plan. Each of these areas focuses on a variety of constituencies—businesses, foundations, organizations, and individuals for annual and capital campaigns; planned giving is generally focused solely on individual giving.

Various fundraising methods are used in the development program, and the plan should include action steps for individual solicitation, telephone solicitation, direct mail, grant proposals, and special events. It is important to have an integrated plan that uses a multitude of approaches, eliminating the dangerous position of having the organization dependent on a single source of funding.

The written planning document should have a narrative that explains the assessment and how the organization arrived at its goals, objectives, and strategies, as well as a detailed task list that includes benchmarking areas of budget, timeline, and areas of responsibility.

The board and CEO should approve the overarching goals of the plan before the development office determines the more detailed aspects of the plan that will be used to achieve these goals.

Further Reading

Lysakowski, Linda. *Recruiting and Training Fundraising Volunteers* (Hoboken, N.J.: John Wiley & Sons, 2005).

Rosso, Henry. *Achieving Excellence in Fundraising: A Comprehensive Guide to Principles, Strategies, and Methods* (San Francisco: Jossey-Bass, 1991).

Seiler, Timothy L. *Developing Your Case for Support* (San Francisco: Jossey-Bass, 2001).

EXHIBIT 5.1

Development Audit & Plan

for

XYZ Organization

December 5, 2000

presented by

CAPITAL VENTURE

P.O. Box 731
Reading, PA 19607
866-539-9990 toll free
linda@cvfundraising.com
www.cvfundraising.com

continued on the next page

Introduction and Methodology

CAPITAL VENTURE was retained to conduct a development audit and construct a development plan for the XYZ Organization. The principal goals of this audit and plan were to:

- Determine if the current staffing of the development office is adequate and to suggest a staffing structure;

- Determine the level of involvement of the associates board and other volunteers in the development program and to make recommendations for the recruitment, training, and involvement of volunteers in the development process;

- Assess the infrastructure currently in place in the development office and suggest improvements to the infrastructure that will enhance the capabilities of the development office in the future;

- Evaluate the current and past fundraising and public relations activities of XYZ Organization and make recommendations for an integrated development program;

- Assess future needs of the organization and recommend strategies for funding these needs.

Linda Lysakowski, ACFRE, principal of CAPITAL VENTURE, met on numerous occasions with the director of development and the executive director. In addition, discussions were held with several board members about the needs of the organization and the proposed goals and objectives. Joe Jones, CAPITAL VENTURE donor database consultant, also met with staff to evaluate the current systems and make recommendations.

The final plan was presented to the associates board at the January board retreat.

Section I Organizational Structure and Operation

Name of Organization: **XYZ Corporation**
Address: **123 Any Road**
                          My Town, PA 12345
Phone: **123-456-7890**
Fax: **123-456-7890**
E-mail: **me@anywhere.com**

Person Responsible for Completion of
Audit Report Information: **Sue Smith**

CAPITAL VENTURE Staff Completing Report: **Linda Lysakowski, ACFRE**

Legal Requirements for Fundraising: The XYZ Organization has 501(c)3 status and is registered with the state of XXX. Since the organization does fundraising in other states as well, there needs to be an assessment of whether any of these other states require registration.

Mission: The XYZ organization, a living history village, collects, preserves and interprets the history and material culture of this part of the country.

Strengths: The mission is clear concise and well written.
Weaknesses: A little wordy in the last part of the sentence.
Recommendations: **Put mission statement on all newsletters, brochures, annual reports, and other constituent communications. Put the mission statement on the back of business cards of staff and at the top of each board meeting agenda.**

Vision: By 2006 XYZ organization will have a well-defined public image that articulates and promotes it mission. It will be major tourist destination site in My Town, serving approximately 150,000 visitors each year based upon annual visitor increases of 25 percent per year. People will visit the organization because of its tranquil setting and

continued on the next page

extensive collections, but also because it is entertaining and informative. It will be an active resource for the local community, especially schools. A professional and competent staff composed of approximately 100 full and part-time positions will serve XYZ Organization. The site will have a budget from all sources in excess of $3,000,000 per year.

Strengths: The vision is clearly defined, realistic, and has measurable objectives with a definite timeline.

Recommendations: **All planning should be done in light of the vision statement, and the progress on the stated goals should be evaluated quarterly.**

Long-Range Organizational Plan

Strengths: Like the vision statement, the business plan has been well thought out, with measurable goals and objectives and a realistic timeline and budget.

Weaknesses: Current staffing maybe inadequate to implement plan fully.

Recommendations: **The organization needs to implement an organization-wide long-range strategic plan involving all areas of the organization— finances, facilities, public relations, program, development, staffing, and governance. This plan must include funding and financing issues in order to assure staffing and resources necessary to implement the plan to its fullest extent.**

Case for Support

Strengths: There is a case for support document in place.

Weaknesses: This case for support needs to be expanded upon to further develop opportunities for participation by donors.

Recommendations: **Develop a case for support for XYZ Organization and individual case statements for the annual fund, capital, and planned giving programs as needed.**

Gift Acceptance Policies Guidelines
  Strengths:
  Weaknesses: None in place.
  Recommendations: **Develop gift acceptance policies before a major capital campaign or planned giving program is implemented.**

Section II Governance

Size of Board: 19 board members
  Strengths: Board size is large enough to appoint committees.
  Weaknesses: Board could be larger; there is also a public perception (perhaps shared by some board members) that because ABC governs the XYZ Organization, they also provide full financial support.
  Recommendations: **Increase number of board members to 25 to 30.**

Demographics of Board
  Strengths: Good mix of male/female and age groups.
  Weaknesses: Could have more ethnic diversity.
  Recommendations: **Actively recruit more ethnically diverse board members if they fit the criteria for board membership.**

Skills/Talents of Board
  Strengths: Good public relations skills, and knowledge of organization's service area.

continued on the next page

Weaknesses: Could use more people with planning and fundraising skills.

Recommendations: **Look for additional board members with fundraising and planning skills, make sure members with legal expertise are replaced when terms expire with other board members with legal expertise.**

Involvement of Board
  Strengths:
  Weaknesses: Board is not involved with fundraising activities.

  Recommendations: **Form a strong development committee of the board; educate this committee to lead the board's fundraising efforts. Initiate board orientation program and position descriptions with expectation for board members. These expectations should include involvement in committees, attendance at meetings, and involvement in fundraising—give and get!**

Financial Commitment of Board
  Strengths: A large percentage of the board has contributed to XYZ.
  Weaknesses: Board has not participated 100 percent in giving to the organization; average board gift is low.

  Recommendations: **Implement a board appeal early in the fiscal year before the year-end mailing or other approaches to the community are implemented. The board should be the first group approached for any fundraising efforts.**

Organization of Board
   Strengths:
   Weaknesses: No board organization chart, committees are not active and involved.
   Recommendations: **Select a key person on the board to serve as chair of the board development committee, develop an organizational chart and expectations for board members and committee members. Enlist strong committee members from inside and outside the board to serve on committees. Invite members of the advisory board to serve on board committees.**

Section III The Development Office

Staffing
   Strengths: Committed staff with marketing, public relations and business skills; performance measures have been outlined.
   Weaknesses: Director of Development is not experienced in nonprofit fundraising; not enough staff.
   Recommendations: **Obtain training for director of development, apply for membership in AFP, investigate attendance at conferences and seminars; increase size of development staff; need a database manager for development and membership.**
Volunteers
   Strengths: Have 500 organization volunteers; advisory council has been disbanded, however all the members of the advisory council have agreed to remain involved.

continued on the next page

123

Weaknesses: Few volunteers serving on board committees, volunteers not used in fundraising activities.

Recommendations: **Define the role of board committees and recruit the appropriate members for these groups. Recruit volunteers to help with fundraising.**

Facilities and Equipment

Strengths: Have a large number of donors/prospects and volunteer staff to manage database.

Weaknesses: No donor database, currently all names are in ACCESS and are in separate databases for different programs.

Recommendations: **Purchase a donor database, assemble all lists into the master database, and hire a staff person to be the database manager. Segment donors by various programs and ability to give. Use database for personalized appeals and all other mailings.**

Interaction with Other Departments

Strengths: Development office reports directly to executive director, and executive director is involved with fundraising activities and plans. Executive director's job description includes fundraising.

Weaknesses: Membership and fundraising events should fall under the development office.

Recommendations: **Make sure all fundraising events and programs fall under the development office. (See Section VI, Special Events).**

Procedures

Strengths:

Weaknesses: No procedure manual in place.

Recommendations: **Develop a procedure manual for receiving, recording, acknowledging and reporting gifts.**

Development Plan
    Strengths: This process will include a plan.
    Weaknesses: No plan in place currently.
    Recommendations: **Develop and implement plan.**

Section IV Development Results and Cost Ratios

Donor/Constituent Ratio: 214:98 last year
Results/Goals Ratio: $21,650: $20,500 last year
Average Gift: $220 last year
Cost Ratio/Return on Investment: 1:14 last year

    Strengths: Number of members increased over past two years, average gift high.
    Weaknesses: Number of donors decreased over past year, rate of return low
    Recommendations: **Increase the number of donors by developing an integrated development program.**

Section V Annual Giving

Board Appeal
    Strengths: Most board members have given.
    Weaknesses: Not 100 percent of board gave to annual fund; low average gift from board, no board goal has been set.
    Recommendations: **Develop board appeal program to be done as the first step in the fundraising plan each year.**

Individual—Personal Solicitation
    Strengths: Receive gifts through givingcapital.com but this program has not been marketed.
    Weaknesses: No individual solicitations are done.
    Recommendations: **Start major gifts program using individual solicitations.**

continued on the next page

Individual—Phone Appeals

    Strengths:

    Weaknesses: None done to date.

    Recommendations: **Implement phonathon for current members.**

Individual—Mail Appeals

    Strengths: Raised over 200 percent of goal two years ago, average gift size high

    Weaknesses: Dropped to 91 percent of goal last year, number of donors dropped, used mass-produced "Dear Friend" letter.

    Recommendations: **Develop strong mail appeal using personalized appeals to various constituents.**

Business/Corporate

    Strengths:

    Weaknesses: Small number of corporate gifts, no formal corporate appeal.

    Recommendations: **Develop an annual business appeal; invite businesses to attend cultivation events throughout the year, involve businesses in events and programs.**

Foundation Grants

    Strengths: Hired grant writer this year, set high goal.

    Weakness: No grants past two years.

    Recommendations: **Continue to develop foundation grants.**

Organizations

    Strengths: Have a speaker's bureau in place and a brochure, have done limited marketing to organizations.

    Weaknesses: No formal, structured process to approach organizations.

Recommendations: **Update brochure, refine organization prospect list and do a targeted mailing to various organizations, cultivate organizations for individual appeals in focused areas.**

Section VI Special Events

Strengths: A number of successful events were held, all went over goal this year, and some have cost ratios of 50 percent or less.

Weaknesses: Some cost ratios are well over 50 percent, large number of events, volunteers/staff time may be draining

Recommendations: **Define events as either program activities or fundraising events and coordinate all fundraising events under the development office and program events under the program staff. Evaluate events and possibly eliminate/combine some events; develop a plan for follow up with attendees at events. Outsource some events by using an event manager to bring in outside groups that would run their own events and pay the organization a rental fee.**

Section VII Prospect Identification and Cultivation

Strengths: Good acknowledgement letters

Weaknesses: No time spent on research, cultivation; thank you letters sent seven days after gifts are received

Recommendations: **Implement a major gift appeal strategy to identify and cultivate major donors; initiate**

continued on the next page

127

a formal research program; send acknowledgement letters within 24 hours of receipt
of gift.

Section VIII Planned Giving

Strengths:
Weaknesses: None done to date.
Recommendations: **Implement a process to identify, cultivate
and solicit planned gifts.**

Section IX Capital Campaigns

Strengths: A partially successful campaign was run several years ago.
Weaknesses: No infrastructure in place to prepare for
capital campaign; board involvement in
previous capital campaign was minimal;
goal was not reached; timeline of campaign
was too long.
Recommendations: **This plan will address internal readiness to
conduct a campaign; conduct a planning
study in preparation for a campaign.**

Section X Donor Recognition

Strengths:
Weaknesses: No program in place.
Recommendations: **Establish a recognition program.**

Section XI Public Relations/Communications

Strengths: Press releases, press coverage, media
contacts, media list, photo file and speaker's
bureaus, open house events, PSAs, Web site,

	program brochures, quarterly, and newsletters in place.
Weaknesses:	Speaking engagements are not done on a regular basis, focus groups not used, no fundraising brochures, no crisis plan in place.
Recommendations:	**Develop fundraising brochure for year-end appeal, use focus groups in conjunction with marketing plan, develop crisis plan.**

Recommendations

Short-Term Goals

I. Develop an infrastructure capable of supporting short and long-term fundraising goals
   a. Develop a donor database by January 2002
      i. Purchase a donor database designed for fundraising
      ii. Segment current donors/prospects in database
      iii. Establish coding structure
      iv. Hire/train staff to maintain database
   b. Develop adequate staffing structure for development office by March 2002
      i. Develop organizational chart for development office
      ii. Develop job description for staff positions
      iii. Hire assistant for development director
   c. Develop policies and procedures by April 2002
      i. Develop gift acceptance policies and have approved by board
      ii. Develop procedure manual for use in development office

II. Involve board in development efforts
   a. Structure board as fundraising board by January 2002
      i. Develop board organizational chart to include board re-sources committee and development committee
      ii. Develop position descriptions for all board members
      iii. Recruit appropriate board members as needed to increase size of Board to 25 to 30 people
   b. Establish development committee as the group that will lead fundraising efforts of Board by January 2002
      i. Develop position description for development committee
      ii. Recruit active members of development committee from board, advisory board and non–board constituency

      iii. Appoint a chairperson of the development committee before the January 26 board retreat

      iv. Have development committee affirm development plan and enlist board's help in implementing plan

III. Develop appropriate fundraising materials

    a. Develop case for support for the XYZ Corporation by January 2002

      i. Review current document as a basis for case statement

      ii. Draft organizational case for support

    b. Develop case statement for annual giving which includes an annual fund goal

      i. Develop levels of giving and giving opportunities

      ii. Prepare draft case statement for annual fund

    c. Develop brochures and other materials to be used in annual appeal

      i. Design brochures, pledge cards, response envelopes, etc.

IV. Develop an integrated plan to approach all constituencies

    a. Segment various constituencies for separate appeals to each constituency by March 2002

      i. Segment constituencies into interest groups

    b. Develop a subcommittee to work on each appeal by May 2002

      i. Enlist the help of advisory council/development committee/board to identify approaches for each constituency

    c. Develop appropriate materials to be used in each appeal by June 2002

      i. Draft letters based on each constituency interest

      ii. Prepare special materials to be used with each group

    d. Implement an appeal to various constituencies through personal solicitation, phonathon and direct mail by July 2002

      i. Enlist volunteers from various constituencies to help with phonathons

continued on the next page

e. Develop and implement cultivation strategies for each constituency by July 2002

  i. Plan cultivation events for each constituency based on a specific funding project for each group

Long Term Goals:

I. Develop a capital campaign to finance long-term capital projects

  a. Develop a case for support for capital campaign by July 2002

  b. Conduct a planning study to assess community readiness to conduct campaign by November 2002

  c. Implement a capital campaign based on the results of the study by January 2003

II. Develop a planned giving program to increase endowment funds

  a. Develop a planned giving society by July 2002

  b. Develop a planned giving prospect list by August 2002

  c. Design planned giving materials by August 2002

  d. Develop relationships with allied professionals who can help implement planned giving program by October 2002

  e. Conduct a planned giving seminar in November 2002

  f. Follow up with planned giving prospect calls as needed starting January 2003

III. Develop a strategic long-range plan for the corporation

  g. Engage the services of a consultant to help with the strategic planning process by February 2002

  h. Review business plan and other departmental plans in place, along with pervious strategic plan by April 2002

  i. Begin planning process by June 2002

Development Plan Detail

		Description	Responsibility	Income	Expenses	Start	End
Goal	**1.0.0**	**INCREASE LONG-TERM FUNDRAISING RESULTS FOR XYZ**					
Objective	**1.1.0**	**Continue major gift appeal started in YYYY by MMM YYYY**					
Tasks	1.1.1	Review YYYY results	XYZ/DD/DC			MM/DD/YYYY	MM/DD/YYYY
	1.1.2	Purge names from YYYY list as appropriate and add from mailing list	DD			MM/DD/YYYY	MM/DD/YYYY
	1.1.3	Hold screening session to acquire additional names	DC/BD/XYZ/DD			MM/DD/YYYY	MM/DD/YYYY
	1.1.4	Add new names to database	DD			MM/DD/YYYY	MM/DD/YYYY
	1.1.5	Hold screening meeting to assign calls	XYZ/DD/CN/ BD/DC			MM/DD/YYYY	MM/DD/YYYY
	1.1.6	Send presolicitation letter to major donor prospects	DD/CN			MM/DD/YYYY	MM/DD/YYYY
	1.1.7	Major gift calls	XYZ/DC/BD			MM/DD/YYYY	MM/DD/YYYY
		Objective subtotal					

continued on the next page

133

	Description	Responsibility	Income	Expenses	Start	End
Objective	**1.2.0 Institute a planned giving program by MMM YYYY**					
Tasks	1.2.1 Prepare a list of professional advisors	CN/XYZ/DD/BD/DC			MM/DD/YYYY	MM/DD/YYYY
	1.2.2 Prepare planned giving brochure	CN/XYZ			MM/DD/YYYY	MM/DD/YYYY
	1.2.3 Prepare information packets for professionals	CN/DD			MM/DD/YYYY	MM/DD/YYYY
	1.2.4 Publish first planned giving article in newsletter	CN/DD			MM/DD/YYYY	MM/DD/YYYY
	1.2.5 Invite professional advisors to breakfast	CN/DD			MM/DD/YYYY	MM/DD/YYYY
	1.2.6 Invite prospective donors to seminar	CN/DD			MM/DD/YYYY	MM/DD/YYYY
	1.2.7 Breakfast	XYZ/BD/DC/DD/CN			MM/DD/YYYY	MM/DD/YYYY
	1.2.8 Planned giving seminar	XYZ/BD/DC/DD/CN			MM/DD/YYYY	MM/DD/YYYY
	1.2.9 Establish planned giving committee	XYZ/DD/CN			MM/DD/YYYY	MM/DD/YYYY
	Objective subtotal					

Objective	**1.3.0**	**Institute a major-gift program by MMM YYYY**					
Tasks	1.3.1	Invite advisory board to victory celebration	XYZ			MM/DD/YYYY	MM/DD/YYYY
	1.3.2	Meet with advisory board to explain project	XYZ/CN			MM/DD/YYYY	MM/DD/YYYY
	1.3.3	Prepare a preliminary prospect list	XYZ/DD/CN			MM/DD/YYYY	MM/DD/YYYY
	1.3.4	Prepare training and solicitation materials	CN			MM/DD/YYYY	MM/DD/YYYY
	1.3.5	Conduct donor screening session	CN/XYZ			MM/DD/YYYY	MM/DD/YYYY
	1.3.6	Assign prospects to solicitors	DD			MM/DD/YYYY	MM/DD/YYYY
	1.3.7	Hold kickoff training meeting	CN/XYZ/DD			MM/DD/YYYY	MM/DD/YYYY
	1.3.8	Conduct solicitation calls	XYZ			MM/DD/YYYY	MM/DD/YYYY
	1.3.9	Report meetings	CN/XYZ/DD			MM/DD/YYYY	MM/DD/YYYY
		Objective subtotal					
Objective	**1.4.0**	**Establish a development office by MMM YYYY**					
Tasks	1.4.1	Establish a full-time development director position	DD			MM/DD/YYYY	MM/DD/YYYY
	1.4.2	Utilize XYZ's time to assist with fundraising efforts—major gift calls	XYZ			MM/DD/YYYY	MM/DD/YYYY

continued on the next page

	Description	Responsibility	Income	Expenses	Start	End
1.4.3	Hire a support staff person	DD			MM/DD/YYYY	MM/DD/YYYY
1.4.4	Operate development office for one year	DD			MM/DD/YYYY	MM/DD/YYYY
	Objective subtotal					
Goal	**2.0.0**	***INCREASE MEMBERSHIP IN XYZ***				
Objective	**2.1.0**	**Continue Year-End Appeal by MMM YYYY**				
Tasks	2.1.1 Review results of YYYY year-end appeal	CN/XYZ/DD			MM/DD/YYYY	MM/DD/YYYY
	2.1.2 Purge mailing list	DD			MM/DD/YYYY	MM/DD/YYYY
	2.1.3 Review and revise case for support with current issues	XYZ/DD/CN			MM/DD/YYYY	MM/DD/YYYY
	2.1.4 Mail pre-phonathon mailing	DD/VL			MM/DD/YYYY	MM/DD/YYYY
	2.1.5 Recruit volunteers	DD/VL			MM/DD/YYYY	MM/DD/YYYY
	2.1.6 Phonathon	DD/CN/XYZ/VL			MM/DD/YYYY	MM/DD/YYYY
	2.1.7 Follow-up mailings	DD			MM/DD/YYYY	MM/DD/YYYY
	Objective subtotal					

Objective	**2.2.0**	**Increase prospect base by acquiring additional mailing lists of potential members by MMM YYYY**				
Tasks	2.2.1	Mail to "hot lists"—create and carry out APC strategy for obtaining/creating hot lists	DD/CN		MM/DD/YYYY	MM/DD/YYYY
	2.2.2	Reprint ABC letter and mini case statement	DD		MM/DD/YYYY	MM/DD/YYYY
	2.2.3	Have volunteers look up phone numbers for "hot lists"	DD		MM/DD/YYYY	MM/DD/YYYY
	2.2.4	Conduct phone appeal to potential new members from list that have phone numbers	CN/DD/XYZ/VL		MM/DD/YYYY	MM/DD/YYYY
	2.2.5	Hold new member brainstorming session to develop potential member lists	XYZ/DD/BD		MM/DD/YYYY	MM/DD/YYYY
		Objective subtotal				
Objective	**2.3.0**	**Plan canvas appeal for membership in MMM YYYY**	**XYZ**		**MM/DD/YYYY**	**MM/DD/YYYY**
Tasks	2.3.1	Enter data from canvas into database	DD		MM/DD/YYYY	MM/DD/YYYY
		Objective subtotal				

continued on the next page

137

	Description	Responsibility	Income	Expenses	Start	End
Objective **2.4.0**	**Conduct membership renewal programs**	**DD**			**MM/DD/YYYY**	**MM/DD/YYYY**
Tasks 2.4.1	Review renewed member lists	DD			MM/DD/YYYY	MM/DD/YYYY
2.4.2	Mail renewal notices	DD			MM/DD/YYYY	MM/DD/YYYY
2.4.3	Mail renewal notices	DD			MM/DD/YYYY	MM/DD/YYYY
2.4.4	Mail renewal notices	DD			MM/DD/YYYY	MM/DD/YYYY
	Objective subtotal					
Goal **3.0.0**	*INCREASE AWARENESS OF XYZ AND ITS WORK*					
Objective **3.1.0**	**Increase circulation and effectiveness of newsletter beginning MMM YYYY**					
Tasks 3.1.1	Insert planned giving articles and development articles in newsletter	CN/XYZ/DD			MM/DD/YYYY	MM/DD/YYYY
3.1.2	Insert response envelopes in newsletter	DD/VL			MM/DD/YYYY	MM/DD/YYYY
	Objective subtotal					
Objective **3.2.0**	**Conduct special events to cultivate donors/members by MMM YYYY**					
Tasks 3.2.1	Hold fundraising dinner	BD/DC/XYZ/DD			MM/DD/YYYY	MM/DD/YYYY

	3.2.2	Conduct plant sale	BD/DC/XYZ/DD		MM/DD/YYYY	MM/DD/YYYY
	3.2.3	Hold members day and silent auction	DD/XYZ/BD/DC		MM/DD/YYYY	MM/DD/YYYY
	3.2.4	Pursue prospect band to hold concert for XYZ	DD		MM/DD/YYYY	MM/DD/YYYY
	3.2.5	Set up exhibit at festival to recruit members	XYZ/DD/DC		MM/DD/YYYY	MM/DD/YYYY
		Objective subtotal				
Objective	**3.3.0**	**Develop relationships with retail outlets and grocery stores to help with fundraising**	DD		MM/DD/YYYY	MM/DD/YYYY
	3.3.1	Identify new outlets for XYZ brochures	DD		MM/DD/YYYY	MM/DD/YYYY
	3.3.2	Increase involvement in community events	BD/DC/XYZ/DD		MM/DD/YYYY	MM/DD/YYYY
		Objective subtotal				
Objective	**3.4.0**	**Increase speaking engagements by board and staff on an ongoing basis**				
Tasks	3.4.1	Develop a list of potential organizations to speak to	BD/DC/XYZ/DD		MM/DD/YYYY	MM/DD/YYYY
	3.4.2	Contact organizations	XYZ/DD/BD/DC		MM/DD/YYYY	MM/DD/YYYY

continued on the next page

139

	Description	Responsibility	Income	Expenses	Start	End
3.4.3	Prepare presentation	DD/XYZ			MM/DD/YYYY	MM/DD/YYYY
3.4.4	Conduct speaking engagements	XYZ/DD/BD/DC			MM/DD/YYYY	MM/DD/YYYY
	Objective subtotal					
Objective	**3.5.0**	**Increase media coverage of XYZ issues and events on an ongoing basis**				
Tasks	3.5.1	Develop a media list focusing on TV, magazines, etc.	DD			MM/DD/YYYY	MM/DD/YYYY
	3.5.2	Prepare a media kit	DD			MM/DD/YYYY	MM/DD/YYYY
	3.5.3	Visit media and deliver kits	XYZ			MM/DD/YYYY	MM/DD/YYYY
	3.5.4	Issue press releases and PSAs as appropriate	XYZ/DD			MM/DD/YYYY	MM/DD/YYYY
	Objective subtotal					
Goal	**4.0.0**	**INCREASE THE ROLE OF THE BOARD IN FUNDRAISING**				
Objective	**4.1.0**	**Increase the size of the Advisory board to ## by MMM YYYY and create executive committee**				
Tasks	4.1.1	Develop a board evaluation grid	CN/XYZ			MM/DD/YYYY	MM/DD/YYYY
	4.1.2	Determine needs of board	CN/XYZ			MM/DD/YYYY	MM/DD/YYYY
	4.1.3	Prepare or revise board job descriptions	CN/XYZ			MM/DD/YYYY	MM/DD/YYYY

	4.1.4	Develop board recruitment packets	CN/XYZ/DD	MM/DD/YYYY	MM/DD/YYYY
	4.1.5	Hold board recruitment strategy meeting	BD/XYZ/CN/DD	MM/DD/YYYY	MM/DD/YYYY
	4.1.6	Recruit new board members and conduct orientation	BC/DR	MM/DD/YYYY	MM/DD/YYYY
		Objective subtotal			
Objective	**4.2.0**	**Continue to involve the board in major and planned giving efforts on an ongoing basis**			
Tasks	4.2.1	Conduct board solicitation as part of major giving program	XYZ/BC	MM/DD/YYYY	MM/DD/YYYY
	4.2.2	Involve board in planned giving program	XYZ/BC	MM/DD/YYYY	MM/DD/YYYY
	4.2.3	Involve board in major gifts program	XYZ/BC	MM/DD/YYYY	MM/DD/YYYY
		Objective subtotal			
Objective	**4.3.0**	**Provide ongoing orientation and training for board members**			
Tasks	4.3.1	Plan board orientation for new and existing board members	XYZ/CN/BC	MM/DD/YYYY	MM/DD/YYYY
	4.3.2	Conduct a strategic planning retreat	XYZ/BC/CN	MM/DD/YYYY	MM/DD/YYYY
		Objective subtotal			

141

Code	Definition	Code	Definition
BD	Advisory board	DC	Development committee
BC	Board chair	DD	Director of development
CN	Consultant	XYZ	XYZ organization
VL	Volunteers		

Development Plan

Short-Range Planning

	Goals, Objectives, and Tasks	Responsibility of	Anticipated Expense	Start Date	End Date
Goal	**1**	**Develop an infrastructure capable of supporting short- and long-term fundraising goals**			
Objective	1.1	Develop a donor database				1/31/02
Tasks	1.1.1	Purchase a donor database designed for fundraising	Smith/Jones	$2,500		12/15/01
	1.1.2	Segment current donors/prospects in database	Smith			1/15/02
	1.1.3	Establish coding structure	Smith/Consultant	$500		1/15/02
	1.1.4	Train staff to use database	Consultant	$500		1/15/02
Objective 1.1		**Anticipated income/expenses**		$3,500		
Objective	1.2	Develop adequate staffing structure for development office	Miller/Jones			
Tasks	1.2.1	Develop organizational chart for development office	Consultant			1/15/02

continued on the next page

	Goals, Objectives, and Tasks	Responsibility of	Anticipated Expense	Start Date	End Date
1.2.2	Develop job descriptions for development staff	Consultant	$250		2/15/02
1.2.3	Hire assistant for development office	Miller/Jones	$30,000		3/15/02
			$30,250		
Objective 1.2	**Anticipated income/expenses**				
Objective 1.3	Develop policies and procedures for development office	Jones/Board			
Tasks 1.3.1	Develop gift acceptance policies and have approved by board	Jones/Consultant	$250		4/15/02
1.3.2	Develop procedure manual for use in development office	Jones/Consultant	$250		3/15/02
			$500		
Objective 1.3	**Anticipated Income/expenses**				
Goal 2	**Involve board in development efforts**				
Objective 2.1	Structure board as a fundraising board	Consultant			11/15/01
Tasks 2.1.1	Develop board organizational chart				
2.1.2	Develop position descriptions for all board members and committees	Miller/Consultant	$250		12/15/01
2.1.3	Recruit board members	Miller/Board			1/15/02
Objective 2.1	**Anticipated income/expenses**		$250		

Objective	2.2	Establish development committee		
Tasks	2.2.1	Develop position descriptions for development committee	Consultant	12/15/01
	2.2.2	Recruit chairperson for development committee	Miller/Jones/Board	1/15/02
	2.2.3	Recruit development committee members	Jones/DC Chair	3/15/02
	2.2.4	Have development committee affirm plan and enlist board's help to implement plan	DC Chair	4/15/02
Objective 2.2		**Anticipated income/expenses**		$500
Goal	**3**	**Develop appropriate fundraising materials**		
Objective	3.1	Develop case for support for XYZ		
Tasks	3.1.1	Review current case for support document	Jones/Consultant	12/15/01
	3.1.2	Draft organizational case	Jones/Consultant	1/15/02
Objective 3.1		**Anticipated income/expenses**		$500
Objective	3.2	Develop case statement for annual giving which includes annual fund goal	Jones/Consultant	

continued on the next page

145

	Goals, Objectives and Tasks	Responsibility of	Anticipated Expense	Start Date	End Date
Tasks	3.2.1 Develop levels of giving and giving opportunities	Jones/Consultant	$500		12/15/01
	3.2.2 Draft annual fund case statement	Jones/Consultant	$500		1/15/02
	Anticipated income/expenses		$1,000		
Objective 3.2					
Objective	3.3 Develop brochures and support materials				
Tasks	3.3.1 Design brochures, pledge cards,. response envelopes, etc	Jones/Consultant	$3,000		1/15/02
	Anticipated income/expenses		$3,000		
Objective 3.3					
Goal	**4 Develop an integrated plan to approach all constituencies**				
Objective	4.1 Segment various constituencies for separate appeals to each constituency				
Tasks	4.1.1 Segment constituencies				1/31/02
	Anticipated income/expenses		$7,000		
Objective 4.1					
Objective	4.2 Develop a subcommittee to work on each constituency appeal	Jones/DC Chair			2/28/02

146

			Responsible	Anticipated income/expenses	Date
Tasks	4.2.1	Enlist the help of board, past advisory board members to identify volunteers and approaches	Jones/DC Chair		03/03/02
Objective 4.2					
Objective	4.3	Develop appropriate materials to be used in constituency appeals	Jones/Consultant	**Anticipated income/expenses** $10,000	
Tasks	4.3.1	Draft letters for each constituency	Consultant	$1,000	5/31/02
	4.3.2	Prepare special materials to be used in various appeals	Consultant	$3,000	6/30/02
Objective 4.3					
Objective	4.4	Implement an appeal to various constituencies using mail, phone and personal visits		**Anticipated income/expenses** $4,000	
Tasks	4.4.1	Enlist volunteers for each constituency	Jones/Dev. Comm.		5/30/02
	4.4.2	Screen prospective donors and select major gift prospects for personal visits	Consultant/Dev. Comm.	$500	6/30/02
	4.4.3	Plan major gift appeal and recruit volunteers	Jones/Dev. Comm./Consultant	$1,000	6/30/02
	4.4.4	Make major gift solicitation visits	Dev. Comm.		11/1/02
	4.4.5	Plan Phonathon and recruit volunteers	Jones/Dev. Comm./Consultant	$1,000	11/15/02

continued on the next page

147

	Goals, Objectives and Tasks	Responsibility of	Anticipated Expense	Start Date	End Date
4.4.6	Send year-end mail appeal	Jones			11/30/02
Objective 4.4	**Anticipated income/expenses**		$2,500		
Objective 4.5	Develop and implement cultivation strategies for each constituency				
Tasks 4.5.1	Plan cultivation events				
4.5.2	Recruit volunteers to host events				
4.5.3	Develop invitation lists				
4.5.4	Hold Cultivation events				
Objective 4.5	**Anticipated income/expenses**	$0			

Long-Range Planning

	Goals, Objectives and Tasks	Responsibility of	Anticipated Expense	Start Date	End Date
Goal 5	**Develop a capital campaign to finance long-term capital projects**				
Objective 5.1	Develop a preliminary case for support for capital campaign including proposed goal	Consultant			7/31/02
Objective 5.2	Conduct a planning study to determine XYZ's readiness to conduct a campaign	Consultant	$18,000		11/30/02
Objective 5.3	Implement a capital campaign based on the results of the board/staff/consultant study		$100,000		7/31/04
Goal 5	**Anticipated income/expenses—long range**		$118,000		

Goal	**6**	**Develop a planned giving program to increase endowment fund**			
Objective	6.1	Develop a planned giving society	Jones/Consultant	$500	7/1/02
Objective	6.2	Develop a planned giving prospect list	Jones/Dev. Comm.		8/30/02
Objective	6.3	Design planned giving materials	Jones/Mark. Co.	$2,000	8/31/02
Objective	6.4	Develop relationships with professionals to help in planned giving program	Jones/Dev. Comm.		10/31/02
Objective	6.5	Conduct a planned giving seminar	Jones/Dev. Comm.	$500	11/30/02
Objective	6.6	Incorporate planned giving into capital campaign	Consultant		1/1/03
Objective	6.7	Follow up with planned giving prospects	Jones/Dev. Comm.		01/01/2003
Goal 6		**Anticipated income/expenses—long range**		$3,000	
Goal 7		**Develop a strategic long-range plan for the organization**			
Objective	7.1	Engage a consultant to help with strategic planning process			2/28/02
Objective	7.2	Review Business plan and other department plans, along with previous strategic plan			11/30/02
Objective	7.3	Begin planning process			6/30/02
Goal 7		**Anticipated income/expenses—long range**		$0	

EXHIBIT 5.2

Large Development Office

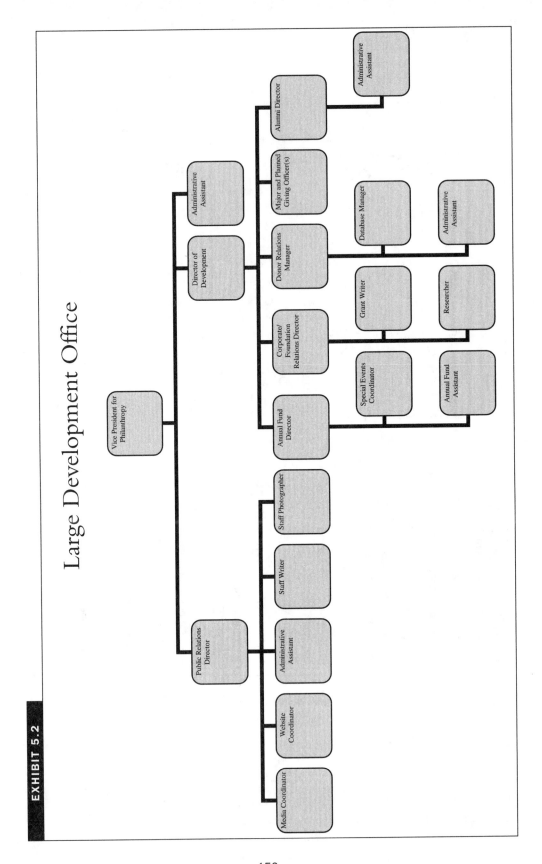

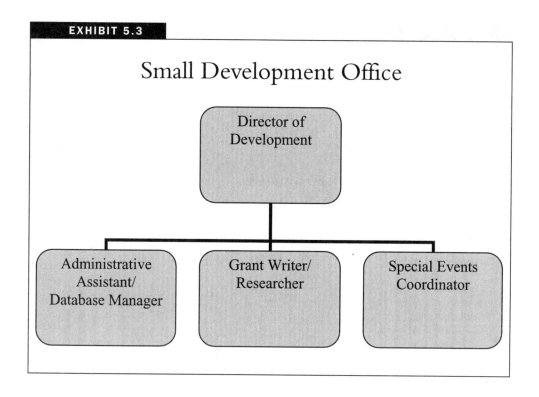

EXHIBIT 5.3

Small Development Office

Director of
Development

Administrative
Assistant/
Database Manager

Grant Writer/
Researcher

Special Events
Coordinator

EXHIBIT 5.4

Potential Donors for Our Organization

Your Name:_____

Category	Name & Address	Potential Major Donor Y or N	I will contact this person Y or N
My accountant			
My car dealer			
My banker(s)			
My attorney			
Members of my professional association			
My insurance agent			
My doctor (s)			
My dentist (s)			
Members of a service club to which I belong			

Category	Name & Address	Potential Major Donor Y or N	I will contact this person Y or N
Neighbors			
Relatives			
Clients/customers of mine			
Politicians I know			

continued on the next page

153

Category	Name & Address	Potential Major Donor Y or N	I will contact this person Y or N
People with whom I worship			
People with whom I work			
People with whom I went to school			

Category	Name & Address	Potential Major Donor Y or N	I will contact this person Y or N
Parents of children with whom my children go to school			
My realtor			
People with whom I do business			
People with whom I play sports			
People I know who support other charities			

continued on the next page

Category	Name & Address	Potential Major Donor Y or N	I will contact this person Y or N
People who have asked me to support their favorite charity			
People I know who volunteer for other nonprofit organizations			
Others			

EXHIBIT 5.5

XYZ Organization

BOARD OF DIRECTORS - FACT SHEET

Name _____ Term Expires _____

Home Address _____ Birth Date _____

Spouse _____ Children _____

Employer _____ _____

Title _____ _____

Business Address _____ _____

Business Phone _____ _____

E-mail address _____ _____

Preferred Mailing Address ☐ Home ☐ Business

Professional Affiliations: _____

_____

_____

Community Activities—other nonprofit boards and committees:

_____

_____

_____

Other Interests: _____

_____

_____

_____

Committee Preference
  ☐ Development ☐ Program ☐ Finance ☐ Planning
  ☐ Board Resource ☐ Special Events ☐ Marketing ☐ Other

Please attach background information or resume (resume preferred) and digital photograph in electronic format.

Please return to:

A Donor Bill of Rights

PHILANTHROPY is based on voluntary action for the common good. It is a tradition of giving and sharing that is primary to the quality of life. To assure that philanthropy merits the respect and trust of the general public, and that donors and prospective donors can have full confidence in the not-for-profit organizations and causes they are asked to support, we declare that all donors have these rights:

I.

To be informed of the organization's mission, of the way the organization intends to use donated resources, and of its capacity to use donations effectively for their intended purposes.

II.

To be informed of the identity of those serving on the organization's governing board, and to expect the board to exercise prudent judgment in its stewardship responsibilities.

III.

To have access to the organization's most recent financial statements.

IV.

To be assured their gifts will be used for the purposes for which they were given.

V.

To receive appropriate acknowledgment and recognition.

VI.

To be assured that information about their donations is handled with respect and with confidentiality to the extent provided by law.

VII.

To expect that all relationships with individuals representing organizations of interest to the donor will be professional in nature.

VIII.

To be informed whether those seeking donations are volunteers, employees of the organization, or hired solicitors.

IX.

To have the opportunity for their names to be deleted from mailing lists that an organization may intend to share.

X.

To feel free to ask questions when making a donation and to receive prompt, truthful and forthright answers.

DEVELOPED BY
Association for Healthcare Philanthropy (AHP)
Association of Fundraising Professionals (AFP)
Council for Advancement & Support of Education (CASE)
Giving Institute: Leading Consultants to Non-Profits

ENDORSED BY
Independent Sector
National Catholic Development Conference (NCDC)
National Committee on Planned Giving (NCPG)
Council for Resource Development (CRD)
United Way of America

CHAPTER 6

Implementing the Plan

"Resolve to take fate by the throat and shake a living out of her."
Louisa May Alcott

After reading this chapter, you will be able to:

- Establish a system of responsibility for implementing the plan.
- Develop a plan to adapt to changes within the organization during the plan implementation phase.
- Develop ways to keep the plan dynamic.

Who Is Responsible for Implementing the Plan?

Now that the plan is written, how does the organization ensure that it will be implemented, monitored, and updated? The chief development officer (CDO) is responsible for monitoring the plan on a regular basis and updating it when necessary.

Regular development office staff meetings should focus on progress of the plan, and any problems need to be discussed in regard to implementing the plan. As stated before, the plan is not written in stone, but neither should it be written in disappearing ink! Included in the plan itself should be a plan to monitor results. At the end of this chapter, there are samples of benchmarking systems based on the previous chapter's samples of the task list (Exhibits 6.1, 6.2, and 6.3). Developing the list in an Access database allows the organization to sort the tasks by dates, budgets, and areas of responsibility. One recommended method for ensuring that the plan is followed is for each person or group responsible for implementing steps to have the tasks sorted by areas of responsibility that belong to their work group so they can focus on their parts of the plan and not get bogged down in what everyone else is doing. However, it will be necessary for the group to meet regularly and review the entire plan in order for each work group to understand how important it is that their section of the plan be implemented in a timely manner, as it affects the rest of the plan.

The CDO can use the timeline as a benchmarking system to monitor progress on a monthly or even weekly basis. A segment of regular staff meetings should be set aside to review progress on the plan.

If there is no development office, the plan may be monitored by the chief executive officer (CEO), a member of the board, or the chair of the development committee. Regardless of who is charged with this duty, there should always be *one* person who assumes the task of monitoring the plan.

How Do Changes within the Organization Affect the Plan?

It has been said that nothing is certain in life except change. Changes will happen within the organization that may affect the development plan, and the development office must be prepared to adapt to these changes.

One of the most serious changes that can affect the plan is if the CDO leaves the organization or is on an extended leave of absence. The monitoring process should include a plan for an alternate person to monitor the plan should this happen. The loss of any key development position will most likely delay certain aspects of the plan unless there is adequate notice given by the departing staff members and the organization is able to fill the vacant positions in a timely manner. Having a good plan in place, however, will make it much easier for the organization to have a smooth transition of a new staff person, whether the position is filled from within or an outside person is hired to fill the vacancy.

The loss of a CEO or board chair can have an equally devastating effect on the development plan, particularly if the organization is involved in a capital campaign. Again, a good succession plan should be in place within the organization so such vacancies can be filled with a minimal amount of internal turmoil. The loss of a CEO or high-profile board member will most likely have more of an effect on the external perception of the organization than the loss of key development staff. Therefore, any parts of the plan that have a dependence on community involvement, such as a capital campaign or a new public awareness campaign, may need to be adjusted.

Other key issues that may affect the plan are budgeting issues within the organization. A loss of a major funding stream may mean that certain areas of the development plan need to be pushed forward or more resources might need to be channeled into new efforts. An unforeseen budget cut may result in delays to parts of the plan that have a large expenditure attached to them—for example, the purchase of a new software system. The person responsible for implementing the plan needs to look at how this new development will affect the overall plan and make adjustments accordingly.

Major scandals, unfortunately, are becoming more prevalent in the nonprofit world. A drastic change within the organization may result from issues of embezzlement, client abuse, or other serious ethical breaches within the organization. If the organization faces a scandal, the plan will undoubtedly suffer along with every other area of the organization's work. This may be the time to focus development efforts inward, strengthening the infrastructure, increasing board involvement and board giving, making staff changes, and so on, rather than attempting a major public fundraising effort.

Natural disasters, as we've seen in recent years, can also have a negative effect on the development plan. The development office itself can be left vulnerable to things like floods, earthquakes, and other major natural disasters. Or there can be a major increase in the demand for funding for organizations that deal with serving victims of these disasters. The organization should have a crisis plan to cover both natural and human-made disasters, and this crisis plan should be carried over into the development plan. For example, donor records should always be backed up and stored in a secure place, perhaps an off-site server.

Not all changes, however, are negative ones. A new CEO, new board leadership, or new development staff can bring a renewed interest in and enthusiasm for development and/or new fundraising skills. Even a disaster or a scandal can sometimes be beneficial to the organization's fundraising efforts.

 IN THE REAL WORLD

A number of years ago, several museums were in the public spotlight because of decisions to sell off parts of their collections and use the money for operating expenses, which violates the American Association of Museums ethical standards. One such museum capitalized on a negative by turning it into a positive. After a high-profile court case determined that the artwork be returned to the museum, the board and staff decided to hold a big "welcome back the paintings" open house event. The event drew hundreds of people to the museum, many who had never been into the art gallery before, and resulted in a very successful fund drive, which followed the event.

TIPS & TECHNIQUES

The Crisis Plan

Every nonprofit should have a crisis plan that establishes guidelines for both physical catastrophes and public scandals. Some points to include in the crisis plan are:

- One person to serve as a spokesperson for the organization.

- Names and phone numbers of media to contact (a proactive stance is better than a reactive one).

- A plan for conducting operations off site in the case of a physical disaster that makes the facility inoperable.

- Back-up storage of important files and records.

- Names and phone numbers of all emergency agencies, such as fire and police.

- A succession plan if key people are out of the picture.

- A financial reserve fund in case operating cash is not available.

Keeping the Plan Dynamic

How does the organization keep the plan alive? Too often, a lot of time and money is spent on developing the plan and then it sits on a shelf gathering dust or is pulled out at the end of the year to see how many goals were met before the organization starts the next cycle of planning. The plan must be a vital, living, breathing part of the development operation.

The benchmarking tools discussed in the next chapter will address how the evaluation process can help the plan dynamic. Assuring that there is a person and a process to evaluate the plan on a regular basis is one way of keeping it alive. Having buy-in from the beginning on the part of every person or group who will be responsible for implementing any part of the plan is another way to ensure that it is a vital living document.

It is also important to remember that the plan cannot be so rigid that it cannot be adapted to changing circumstances, while at the same time taking the deadlines seriously. Setting goals that are realistic is another key to keeping the document dynamic, but the organization must be careful not to fall into the trap of setting standards so low that they are easily achieved or not worth working toward.

The document itself also must be easy to read and follow, and preferably something that can be easily translated into a PowerPoint slide show that can be reviewed at staff meetings or a Gantt chart that can be posted in each staff person's work space. Lively discussion of the plan at staff, board, and development committee meetings will also keep the plan alive.

 TIPS & TECHNIQUES

Keeping the Plan Alive

Some keys to keeping the plan alive:

- Make sure all parties have buy-in from the very beginning on the goals, objectives, and strategies.

- Establish realistic goals and objectives to keep people from becoming frustrated because goals are not reached.

- Assign a person to monitor the plan.

- Establish a benchmarking system to assess progress.

- Follow deadlines—keep a calendar in a prominent location so that everyone can follow it.

- Plan regular report meetings where everyone involved reports on progress and explains any discrepancies in meeting deadlines and/or budgets.

- Celebrate success.

Summary

There must be one person responsible for monitoring the plan, although the entire development staff, the CEO, the board, and volunteers must all be held accountable for their portions of the plan.

There will be changes within the organization that will affect the development plan. These can include:

- Loss of key development staff, CEO, or a key board member.

- New development staff, CEO, or board members.

- Budget cuts within the organization.

- Scandal.

- Natural disasters.

The development plan should be flexible enough to handle these changes, whether they have negative or positive effects on the organization.

The organization must have a crisis plan in effect in order to deal with major disasters, either natural catastrophes or public scandal.

The plan can be kept dynamic if the organization:

- Obtains buy-in on the goals, objectives, and strategies of the plan from all people and groups who will be involved in implementing the plan.

- Establishes realistic goals.

- Assigns someone to monitor the plan and establishes a benchmarking system.

- Recognizes failings and adjusts the plan as necessary.

- Celebrates success and discusses ways to build on that success.

EXHIBIT 6.1

Budget Detail by Date

Ref. #	Task Detail	Income	Expenses	Timeline Start Date	End Date	Status
4.1.3	Place ads for CDO position		$500	1/2/2002	1/7/2002	Completed
1.2.4	Conduct board solicitations	$10,000		2/10/2002	3/25/2002	
1.1.6	Prepare appropriate materials from case		2,500	3/15/2002	4/30/2002	
1.3.5	Prepare major-gift appeal materials		100	4/1/2002	5/30/2002	
2.5.3	Join selected organizations		2,000	5/1/2002	5/31/2002	
1.4.4	Look up phone numbers of phonathon prospects		500	6/1/2002	6/30/2002	
2.5.4	Participate in organization activities		500	6/1/2002	12/31/2002	
1.3.7	Solicit major gifts	50,000		6/15/2002	9/30/2002	
1.5.3	Hold dance party event	40,000	10,000	6/22/2002	6/22/2002	
2.1.4	Hold first business leaders breakfast		200	7/1/2002	7/31/2002	
2.2.7	Seek funding for video	10,000		7/1/2002	8/31/2002	
2.3.3	Have publicity materials printed		5,000	7/1/2002	8/31/2002	
2.4.4	Prepare a letter and flyer to be mailed to organizations		200	8/1/2002	8/31/2002	
1.4.8	Mail pre-phonathon letter		200	8/10/2002	8/15/2002	
1.4.9	Conduct phonathon	10,000		8/15/2002	8/31/2002	
1.4.10	Mail follow-up letters		500	8/31/2002	9/5/2002	
2.1.6	Continue to hold business leaders breakfasts monthly or quarterly		1,000	9/1/2002		Ongoing
2.2.8	Produce video		10,000	9/1/2002	12/31/2002	
2.4.7	Mail letters about speakers' bureau to organizations		100	9/15/2002	9/30/2002	
		$120,000	$33,333			

EXHIBIT 6.2

Task by Date

Ref. #	Task Detail	Timeline		Status
		Start Date	End Date	
1.1.1	Review current case for support	12/1/2001	12/15/2001	Completed
4.1.1	Develop position description for CDO	12/1/2001	12/31/2001	Completed
3.2.1	Review current board expectations	12/1/2001	12/31/2001	Completed
4.1.2	Develop list of places to advertise for CDO	12/1/2001	12/31/2001	Completed
1.1.2	Prepare draft of case for support	1/2/2002	1/31/2001	Completed
4.1.3	Place ads for CDO position	1/2/2002	1/7/2002	Completed
1.2.1	Appoint Board Appeal Committee	1/8/2002	1/30/2002	Completed
3.2.2	Prepare proposed board expectations	1/10/2002	1/31/2002	Completed
4.1.4	Receive and screen applicants for CDO position	1/10/2002	2/10/2002	Completed
1.5.1	Assess previous events and determine which event(s) to hold in 2002	1/10/2002	2/15/2002	Completed
3.1.1	Endorse development plan	1/28/2002	1/28/2002	Completed
1.4.1	Develop proposed membership levels	2/1/2002	2/6/2002	Completed
1.5.2	Recruit committee to plan event	2/1/2002	2/15/2002	
2.2.1	Plan Web site	2/1/2002	2/28/2002	Completed
2.2.3	Investigate billboard opportunities	2/1/2002	2/28/2002	
1.3.1	Develop a preliminary major-gift prospect list	2/1/2002	3/31/2002	
1.3.2	Develop recognition program for major gifts	2/1/2002	3/31/2002	
1.1.3	Review draft of case for support	2/7/2002	2/7/2002	Completed
1.2.2	Conduct board screening session	2/7/2002	2/7/2002	Completed
1.2.3	Send board appeal letter	2/8/2002	2/10/2002	Completed
1.1.4	Finalize case for support	2/8/2002	3/15/2002	
4.1.5	Conduct initial interviews for CDO applicants	2/10/2002	2/20/2002	Completed
1.2.4	Conduct board solicitations	2/10/2002	3/25/2002	
4.1.6	Make initial recommendations for CDO to Board	2/20/2002	2/28/2002	Completed
4.3.2	Develop a position description for development committee	3/1/2002	3/20/2002	

continued on the next page

		Timeline		
Ref. #	Task Detail	Start Date	End Date	Status
4.1.7	Conduct final interviews for CDO	3/1/2002	3/31/2002	
2.5.1	Prepare a list of potential organizations to join	3/1/2002	3/31/2002	
2.3.1	Determine publicity materials needed	3/1/2002	4/30/2002	
2.1.1	Develop prospect list for business leaders breakfast	3/1/2002	4/30/2002	
4.3.3	Develop a list of potential development committee members	3/1/2002	4/30/2002	
3.1.2	Develop and implement awareness survey	3/1/2002	5/31/2002	
2.2.4	Issue news releases	3/1/2002	12/31/2002	
1.1.6	Prepare appropriate materials from case	3/15/2002	4/30/2002	
3.2.3	Approve board expectations	3/25/2002	3/25/2002	
1.1.5	Endorse case for support	3/25/2002	3/25/2002	
4.1.8	Make offer to top CDO candidate	4/1/2002	4/10/2002	
2.5.2	Investigate cost and benefits of organizations	4/1/2002	4/30/2002	
1.3.3	Recruit volunteers to help with major-gift appeal	4/1/2002	5/1/2002	
1.3.4	Conduct screening meeting	4/1/2002	5/15/2002	
1.3.5	Prepare major-gift appeal materials	4/1/2002	5/30/2002	
2.2.2	Design and install Web site	4/1/2002	5/31/2002	
4.3.4	Invite potential development committee members to an orientation meeting	5/1/2002	5/30/2002	
4.3.1	Appoint a board member to chair the development committee	5/1/2002	5/30/2002	
1.4.3	Investigate rental or purchase of prospect lists	5/1/2002	5/31/2002	
1.4.2	Segment donor/prospect lists to determine approach for various prospects	5/1/2002	5/31/2002	
2.5.3	Join selected organizations	5/1/2002	5/31/2002	
2.1.2	Prepare agenda and materials for business leaders breakfast	5/1/2002	5/31/2002	
2.2.6	Investigate video needs and opportunities	5/1/2002	6/30/2002	
2.3.2	Design publicity materials	5/1/2002	6/30/2002	

Ref. #	Task Detail	Timeline		Status
		Start Date	End Date	
1.3.6	Conduct board training meeting	6/1/2002	6/15/2002	
1.4.5	Schedule phonathon and secure location	6/1/2002	6/30/2002	
4.3.5	Recruit development committee members	6/1/2002	6/30/2002	
3.1.3	Evaluate awareness survey	6/1/2002	6/30/2002	
1.4.4	Look up phone numbers of phonathon prospects	6/1/2002	6/30/2002	
2.5.4	Participate in organization activities	6/1/2002	12/31/2002	
2.1.3	Invite prospective business leaders to first business leaders breakfast	6/15/2002	7/1/2002	
1.3.7	Solicit major gifts	6/15/2002	9/30/2002	
1.5.3	Hold dance party event	6/22/2002	6/22/2002	
1.4.6	Recruit phonathon volunteers	7/1/2002	7/31/2002	
2.1.4	Hold first business leaders breakfast	7/1/2002	7/31/2002	
4.3.6	Hold first development committee meeting	7/1/2002	7/31/2002	
4.2.1	Do analysis of past years' thrift shop income	7/1/2002	7/31/2002	
2.4.1	Develop a list of organizations for speaking engagements	7/1/2002	7/31/2002	
2.4.2	Develop a list of potential speakers	7/1/2002	7/31/2002	
4.2.2	Investigate other thrift shops to see what their success factors are	7/1/2002	8/31/2002	
2.3.3	Have publicity materials printed	7/1/2002	8/31/2002	
2.2.7	Seek funding for video	7/1/2002	8/31/2002	
4.4.1	Develop a case for support for planned giving	7/1/2002	9/30/2002	
1.4.7	Prepare phonathon materials	8/1/2002	8/15/2002	
2.4.5	Prepare PPT show for speakers	8/1/2002	8/30/2002	
3.1.5	Identify tag line for public awareness	8/1/2002	8/30/2002	
3.1.4	Evaluate success of cultivation events in raising awareness	8/1/2002	8/31/2002	
2.4.3	Recruit speakers for speakers' bureau	8/1/2002	8/31/2002	
2.1.5	Evaluate results of first business leaders breakfast	8/1/2002	8/31/2002	
2.4.4	Prepare a letter and flyer to be mailed to organizations	8/1/2002	8/31/2002	
4.4.2	Develop a list of potential planned giving committee members	8/1/2002	9/30/2002	
1.4.8	Mail pre-phonathon letter	8/10/2002	8/15/2002	

continued on the next page

		Timeline		
Ref. #	Task Detail	Start Date	End Date	Status
1.4.9	Conduct phonathon	8/15/2002	8/31/2002	
1.4.10	Mail follow-up letters	8/31/2002	9/5/2002	
2.1.6	Continue to hold business leaders breakfasts monthly or quarterly	9/1/2002		Ongoing
2.4.6	Hold training meeting for speakers	9/1/2002	9/15/2002	
4.2.3	Evaluate location options for thrift shops	9/1/2002	10/31/2002	
4.4.4	Develop planned giving materials	9/1/2002	12/31/2002	
4.4.3	Develop a list of allied planned giving professionals to cultivate and educate	9/1/2002	12/31/2002	
2.2.8	Produce video	9/1/2002	12/31/2002	
2.4.7	Mail letters about speakers' bureau to organizations	9/15/2002	9/30/2002	
2.4.8	Conduct speaking engagements	10/1/2002		Ongoing
4.2.4	Develop a plan to increase revenue of thrift shop	10/1/2002	11/30/2002	
4.4.5	Launch planned giving program	1/1/2003	12/31/2003	

EXHIBIT 6.3

Tasks by Area of Responsibility

Board Chair

Ref. #	Task Detail	Responsibility of	Start Date	End Date	Status
1.2.1	Appoint board appeal committee	BC ED	1/8/2002	1/30/2002	Completed
1.2.3	Send board appeal letter	CV BC	2/8/2002	2/10/2002	Completed

Board of Directors

Ref. #	Task Detail	Responsibility of	Start Date	End Date	Status
3.1.1	Endorse development plan	BD	1/28/2002	1/28/2002	Completed
1.5.2	Recruit committee to plan event	DD BD	2/1/2002	2/15/2002	
4.1.7	Conduct final interviews for CDO	RDT BD	3/1/2002	3/31/2002	
2.1.1	Develop prospect list for business leaders breakfast	RDT BD	3/1/2002	4/30/2002	
4.3.3	Develop a list of potential development committee members	CDO DD BD	3/1/2002	4/30/2002	
3.1.2	Develop and implement awareness survey	BD	3/1/2002	5/31/2002	
3.2.3	Approve board expectations	BD	3/25/2002	3/25/2002	

continued on the next page

Ref. #	Task Detail	Responsibility of	Timeline		Status
			Start Date	End Date	
1.1.5	Endorse case for support	BD	3/25/2002	3/25/2002	
1.3.3	Recruit volunteers to help with major-gift appeal	BD	4/1/2002	5/1/2002	
4.3.4	Invite potential development Committee members to an orientation meeting	CDO DD BD	5/1/2002	5/30/2002	
3.1.3	Evaluate awareness survey	BD RDT	6/1/2002	6/30/2002	
4.3.5	Recruit development committee members	CDO DD BD	6/1/2002	6/30/2002	
2.1.3	Invite prospective business leaders to first business leaders breakfast	DD BD	6/15/2002	7/1/2002	
1.3.7	Solicit major gifts	BD VL	6/15/2002	9/30/2002	
2.1.4	Hold first business leaders breakfast	RDT BD	7/1/2002	7/31/2002	
3.1.5	Identify tag line for public awareness	BD RDT	8/1/2002	8/30/2002	
3.1.4	Evaluate success of cultivation events in raising awareness	BD RDT	8/1/2002	8/31/2002	
2.4.3	Recruit speakers for speakers' bureau	RDT BD	8/1/2002	8/31/2002	
2.1.5	Evaluate results of first business leaders breakfast	RDT BD	8/1/2002	8/31/2002	
2.1.6	Continue to hold business leaders breakfasts monthly or quarterly	RDT BD	9/1/2002		Ongoing

Board Appeal Committee

Ref. #	Task Detail	Responsibility of	Timeline Start Date	End Date	Status
1.2.2	Conduct board screening session	CV BAC	2/7/2002	2/7/2002	Completed
1.2.4	Conduct board solicitations	BAC	2/10/2002	3/25/2002	

Development Consulting Firm

Ref. #	Task Detail	Responsibility of	Timeline Start Date	End Date	Status
1.1.1	Review current case for support	CV	12/1/2001	12/15/2001	Completed
4.1.1	Develop position description for CDO	CV	12/1/2001	12/31/2001	Completed
3.2.1	Review current board expectations	CV	12/1/2001	12/31/2001	Completed
4.1.3	Place ads for CDO position	CV	1/2/2002	1/7/2002	Completed
3.2.2	Prepare proposed board expectations	CV	1/10/2002	1/31/2002	Completed
4.1.4	Receive and screen applicants for CDO position	CV	1/10/2002	2/10/2002	Completed
1.4.1	Develop proposed membership levels	CV	2/1/2002	2/6/2002	Completed
1.2.2	Conduct board screening session	CV BAC	2/7/2002	2/7/2002	Completed
1.2.3	Send board appeal letter	CV BC	2/8/2002	2/10/2002	Completed
1.1.4	Finalize case for support	DPR CV	2/8/2002	3/15/2002	Completed
4.1.5	Conduct initial interviews for CDO applicants	CV	2/10/2002	2/20/2002	Completed

continued on the next page

Ref. #	Task Detail	Responsibility of	Timeline Start Date	End Date	Status
4.1.6	Make initial recommendations for CDO to board	CV	2/20/2002	2/28/2002	Completed
4.3.2	Develop a position description for development committee	CV	3/1/2002	3/20/2002	
1.1.6	Prepare appropriate materials from case	DPR CV	3/15/2002	4/30/2002	
2.5.2	Investigate cost and benefits of organizations	CV DPR	4/1/2002	4/30/2002	
1.3.4	Conduct screening meeting	CV	4/1/2002	5/15/2002	
1.4.2	Segment donor/prospect lists to determine approach for various prospects	DD CV	5/1/2002	5/31/2002	
2.3.2	Design publicity materials	DPR CV	5/1/2002	6/30/2002	
1.3.6	Conduct board training meeting	CV	6/1/2002	6/15/2002	
1.4.7	Prepare phonathon materials	DD DPR CV	8/1/2002	8/15/2002	
2.4.4	Prepare a letter and flyer to be mailed to organizations	CV DPR	8/1/2002	8/31/2002	
1.4.9	Conduct phonathon	DD CV	8/15/2002	8/31/2002	
2.4.6	Hold training meeting for speakers	CV DPR	9/1/2002	9/15/2002	

Chief Development Officer

Ref. #	Task Detail	Responsibility of	Timeline Start Date	End Date	Status
4.3.3	Develop a list of potential development committee members	CDO DD BD	3/1/2002	4/30/2002	
4.3.4	Invite potential development committee members to an orientation meeting	CDO DD BD	5/1/2002	5/30/2002	

Ref. #	Task Detail	Responsibility of	Timeline Start Date	End Date	Status
4.3.1	Appoint a board member to chair the development committee	CDO DD	5/1/2002	5/30/2002	
1.4.3	Investigate rental or purchase of prospect lists	CDO DD	5/1/2002	5/31/2002	
2.2.6	Investigate video needs and opportunities	DPR CDO	5/1/2002	6/30/2002	
4.3.5	Recruit development committee members	CDO DD BD	6/1/2002	6/30/2002	
2.5.4	Participate in organization activities	ED CDO DD DPR	6/1/2002	12/31/2002	
1.5.3	Hold dance party event	CDO DD EC	6/22/2002	6/22/2002	
4.3.6	Hold first development committee meeting	CDO	7/1/2002	7/31/2002	
4.2.2	Investigate other thrift shops to see what their success factors are	CDO DD	7/1/2002	8/31/2002	
2.2.7	Seek funding for video	CDO	7/1/2002	8/31/2002	
4.4.1	Develop a case for support for planned giving	CDO	7/1/2002	9/30/2002	
4.4.2	Develop a list of potential planned giving committee members	CDO	8/1/2002	9/30/2002	
4.4.3	Develop a list of allied planned giving professionals to cultivate and educate	CDO	9/1/2002	12/31/2002	
4.4.4	Develop planned giving materials	CDO	9/1/2002	12/31/2002	
4.4.5	Launch planned giving program	CDO	1/1/2003	12/31/2003	

Director of Development

Ref. #	Task Detail	Responsibility of	Timeline Start Date	End Date	Status
1.5.2	Recruit committee to plan event	DD BD	2/1/2002	2/15/2002	
4.3.3	Develop a list of potential development committee members	CDO DD BD	3/1/2002	4/30/2002	

continued on the next page

Ref. #	Task Detail	Responsibility of	Timeline Start Date	End Date	Status
4.3.4	Invite potential development committee members to an orientation meeting.	CDO DD BD	5/1/2002	5/30/2002	
4.3.1	Appoint a board member to chair the development committee	CDO DD	5/1/2002	5/30/2002	
1.4.3	Investigate rental or purchase of prospect lists	CDO DD	5/1/2002	5/31/2002	
1.4.2	Segment donor/ prospect lists to determine approach for various prospects	DD CV	5/1/2002	5/31/2002	
1.4.5	Schedule phonathon and secure location	DD	6/1/2002	6/30/2002	
4.3.5	Recruit development committee members	CDO DD BD	6/1/2002	6/30/2002	
2.5.4	Participate in organization activities	ED CDO DD DPR	6/1/2002	12/31/2002	
2.1.1	Invite prospective business leaders to first business leaders breakfast	DD BD	6/15/2002	7/1/2002	
1.5.3	Hold dance party event	CDO DD EC	6/22/2002	6/22/2002	
2.4.2	Develop a list of potential speakers	DD DPR	7/1/2002	7/31/2002	
1.4.6	Recruit phonathon volunteers	DD DPR	7/1/2002	7/31/2002	
4.2.1	Do analysis of past years' thrift shop income	DD	7/1/2002	7/31/2002	
4.2.2	Investigate other thrift shops to see what their success factors are	CDO DD	7/1/2002	8/31/2002	
1.4.7	Prepare phonathon materials	DD DPR CV	8/1/2002	8/15/2002	
1.4.8	Mail pre-phonathon letter	DD	8/10/2002	8/15/2002	
1.4.9	Conduct phonathon	DD CV	8/15/2002	8/31/2002	
1.4.10	Mail follow-up letters	DD	8/31/2002	9/5/2002	

Director of Public Relations

Ref. #	Task Detail	Responsibility of	Timeline Start Date	End Date	Status
1.1.2	Prepare draft of case for support	ED DPR	1/2/2002	1/31/2001	Completed
2.2.1	Plan Web site	DPR	2/1/2002	2/28/2002	Completed
2.2.3	Investigate billboard opportunities	DPR	2/1/2002	2/28/2002	
1.1.4	Finalize case for support	DPR CV	2/8/2002	3/15/2002	
2.2.4	Issue news releases	DPR	3/1/2002	12/31/2002	
1.1.6	Prepare appropriate materials from case	DPR CV	3/15/2002	4/30/2002	
2.5.2	Investigate cost and benefits of organizations	CV DPR	4/1/2002	4/30/2002	
2.3.2	Design publicity materials	DPR CV	5/1/2002	6/30/2002	
2.2.6	Investigate video needs and opportunities	DPR CDO	5/1/2002	6/30/2002	
2.5.4	Participate in organization activities	ED CDO DD DPR	6/1/2002	12/31/2002	
2.4.2	Develop a list of potential speakers	DD DPR	7/1/2002	7/31/2002	
1.4.6	Recruit phonathon volunteers	DD DPR	7/1/2002	7/31/2002	
2.3.3	Have publicity materials printed	DPR	7/1/2002	8/31/2002	
1.4.7	Prepare phonathon materials	DD DPR CV	8/1/2002	8/15/2002	
2.4.5	Prepare PPT show for speakers	DPR	8/1/2002	8/30/2002	
2.4.4	Prepare a letter and flyer to be mailed to organizations	CV DPR	8/1/2002	8/31/2002	
2.4.6	Hold training meeting for speakers	CV DPR	9/1/2002	9/15/2002	
2.4.7	Mail letters about speakers' bureau to organizations	DPR	9/15/2002	9/30/2002	

continued on the next page

Event Committee

Ref. #	Task Detail	Responsibility of	Timeline Start Date	End Date	Status
1.5.3	Hold dance party event	CDO DD EC	6/22/2002	6/22/2002	

Executive Director

Ref. #	Task Detail	Responsibility of	Timeline Start Date	End Date	Status
1.1.2	Prepare draft of case for support	ED DPR	1/2/2002	1/31/2001	Completed
1.2.1	Appoint board appeal committee	BC ED	12/31/2002	1/8/2003	Completed
4.1.8	Make offer to top CDO candidate	ED	4/1/2002	4/30/2002	
2.5.4	Participate in organization activities	ED CDO DD DPR	6/1/2002		Ongoing

Outside Consultant

Ref. #	Task Detail	Responsibility of	Timeline Start Date	End Date	Status
2.2.2	Design and install Web site	OC	4/1/2002	5/31/2002	
1.4.4	Look up phone numbers of phonathon prospects	OC	6/1/2002	6/30/2002	
2.2.8	Produce video	OC RDT	9/1/2002	12/31/2002	

Resource Development Team

Ref. #	Task Detail	Responsibility of	Timeline Start Date	End Date	Status
4.1.2	Develop list of places to advertise for CDO	RDT	12/1/2001	12/31/2001	Completed
1.5.1	Assess previous events and determine which event (s) to hold in 2002	RDT	1/10/2002	2/15/2002	Completed

1.3.1	Develop a preliminary major-gift prospect list	RDT	2/1/2002	3/31/2002	
1.3.2	Develop recognition program for major gifts	RDT	2/1/2002	3/31/2002	
1.1.3	Review draft of case for support	RDT	2/7/2002	2/7/2002	Completed
4.1.7	Conduct final interviews for CDO	RDT BD	3/1/2002	3/31/2002	
2.5.1	Prepare a list of potential organizations to join	RDT	3/1/2002	3/31/2002	
2.3.1	Determine publicity materials needed	RDT	3/1/2002	4/30/2002	
2.1.1	Develop prospect list for business leaders breakfast	RDT BD	3/1/2002	4/30/2002	
1.3.5	Prepare major-gift appeal materials	RDT	4/1/2002	5/30/2002	
2.5.3	Join selected organizations	RDT	5/1/2002	5/31/2002	
2.1.2	Prepare agenda and materials for business leaders breakfast	RDT	5/1/2002	5/31/2002	
3.1.3	Evaluate awareness survey	BD RDT	6/1/2002	6/30/2002	
2.1.4	Hold first business leaders breakfast	RDT BD	7/1/2002	7/31/2002	
2.4.1	Develop a list of organizations for speaking engagements	RDT	7/1/2002	7/31/2002	
3.1.5	Identify tag line for public awareness	BD RDT	8/1/2002	8/30/2002	
2.1.5	Evaluate results of first business leaders breakfast	RDT BD	8/1/2002	8/31/2002	
2.4.3	Recruit speakers for speakers' bureau	RDT BD	8/1/2002	8/31/2002	
3.1.4	Evaluate success of cultivation events in raising awareness	BD RDT	8/1/2002	8/31/2002	

continued on the next page

179

Ref. #	Task Detail	Responsibility of	Timeline Start Date	End Date	Status
2.1.6	Continue to hold business leaders breakfasts monthly or quarterly	RDT BD	9/1/2002		Ongoing
4.2.3	Evaluate location options for thrift shops	RDT	9/1/2002	10/31/2002	
2.2.8	Produce video	OC RDT	9/1/2002	12/31/2002	
4.2.4	Develop a plan to increase revenue of thrift shop	RDT	10/1/2002	11/30/2002	

Volunteers

Ref. #	Task Detail	Responsibility of	Timeline Start Date	End Date	Status
1.3.7	Solicit major gifts	BD VL	6/15/2002	9/30/2002	
2.4.8	Conduct speaking engagements	VL	10/1/2002		Ongoing

Responsibility Code and Description

Code	Description	Code	Description
BC	Board chair	DD	Director of development
BAC	Board appeal committee	DPR	Director of public relations
BD	Board of directors	EC	Event committee
BP	Board president	ED	Executive director
CDO	Chief development officer	OC	Outside consultant

CHAPTER 7

Evaluating Success

"It often happens that I wake at night and begin to think about a serious problem and decide I must tell the Pope about it. Then I wake up completely and remember that I am the Pope!"
Pope John XXIII

After reading this chapter, you will be able to:

- Determine what benchmarking strategies will be used in the plan.
- Develop alternatives for getting the plan back on track.
- Develop a system to hold people accountable for their part of the plan.

Benchmarking Strategies

Taking responsibility for implementing and monitoring the plan is not always the easiest task to assume. Often, it is difficult to assume responsibility for something that depends on many other people to implement. How do development officers track success, and how do they deal with the failings, and the successes, of themselves or others in regard to the implementation of the plan?

Fundraising Costs

Benchmarking costs of fundraising is one of the most challenging aspects of the development profession because there are many factors that go into the costs attached to fundraising activities. Development people must look at return on investment (ROI) and not just the cost of the fundraising activities individually and collectively. Although the factors that affect the costs must be taken into account, such as the fundraising history of the organization, the commitment to fundraising on the part of senior staff and board leadership, the number of prospective donors already connected to the organization, and the technology available to the development office. There are some basic guidelines to which the development office can measure its costs. Jim Greenfield includes a chart of average fundraising costs in his book *Fund Raising*:

Reasonable Cost Guidelines for Solicitation Activities	
Solicitation Activity	**Reasonable Cost Guidelines**
Direct mail (acquisition)	$1.25 to $1.50 per $1.00 raised
Direct mail (renewal)	$.20 to $.25 per $1.00 raised
Membership associations	$.20 to $.30 per $1.00 raised
Activities, benefits, and special events	$.50 per $1.00 raised (gross revenue and direct costs only)
Donor clubs and support group organizations	$20 to $.30 per $1.00 raised
Volunteer-led personal solicitation	$.10 to $.20 per dollar raised
Corporations	$.20 per dollar raised
Foundations	$.20 per dollar raised
Special projects	$.10 to $.20 per dollar raised
Capital campaigns	$.10 to $.20 per dollar raised
Planned giving	$.20 to $.30 per dollar raised

Although it may seem confusing to the novice in fundraising that any organization would spend $1.25 to $1.50 to raise $1.00 through a direct mail acquisition, the seasoned professional understands that this method of fundraising is used to build a database for future major gifts. This method of fundraising more than makes sense for organizations that have a plan to cultivate and solicit these first-time donors for multiple future gifts. It is important for the development officer to explain the reasoning behind the various methods of funding that are integral parts of the development plan. And it is equally important for the development officer to monitor costs of each of these methods so they are not totally out of line with acceptable standards.

Since an organization's 990 form is public information, it is likely that donors will also be watching and monitoring the organization's fundraising costs. In fact, there are numerous sources of information for the wise donor that encourage such monitoring. Therefore, it is even more important that the development office track its costs and report them in a truthful manner. Although some of these organizations do not take into account all the factors that influence costs of fundraising, many donors rely on these sources when making giving decisions, so the development office should be aware of these standards and be prepared to justify their own costs if they do not fall within these guidelines. One such measure is the guideline of the federal government's Combined Federal Campaign, which raised nearly $250 million for nonprofits in 2003. The Combined Federal Campaign requires that participating organizations certify that their combined fundraising and administrative costs constitute no more than 25 percent of the organization's total revenues. The Better Business Bureau cites a maximum of 35 percent of revenues spent on fundraising costs as a standard guideline.

The Urban Institute and Indiana University provide a guide for donors, *Donating to Charity: A Guide*, which warns donors that low overhead costs should not be the sole criterion by which to judge charities worthy of their donations. The authors state that, in fact, the "emphasis on low overhead, far from enhancing the efficiency of charitable organizations, has reduced their effectives and corrupted their accounting." The recommendations this reports makes to donors can be translated into what the development office should monitor in the plan. The authors cite the following recommendations to donors:

- Make sure the charity is legitimate.

- Understand the costs of donor acquisition.

- Bigger gifts mean less goes to fundraising costs.

- Understand the costs of different fundraising methods.

The development officer should understand these same concepts and monitor their organization's development program in regard to each of these points.

- Is the organization fully compliant with legal standards for nonprofits in their country, state or province, and local municipality? Does it understand and adhere to the Association of Fundraising Professionals (AFP) Code of Ethics and/or other professional ethical standards?

- Does the organization understand that it costs more money to acquire new donors than it does to raise money from existing donors? While acquisition is important, more efforts should be placed on renewed and increased donations from current donors.

- Does the plan emphasize major gifts fundraising? The 90/10 rule should be understood—90 percent of donations will most likely come from 10 percent of the organization's donors.

- Does it utilize various fundraising methods and budget realistic costs for each of these methods? If one method of fundraising fails, other funding streams can make up the difference.

 IN THE REAL WORLD

One organization tracks its donations on a weekly basis and posts a sign in every development staff member's office that says, "This week 92 percent of our donations came from 8 percent of our donors" (changing the statistic weekly), to keep their staff focused on the importance of major gifts.

TIPS & TECHNIQUES

In the past, the 80/20 rule was in effect, stating that 80 percent of donations tend to be the result of gifts from 20 percent of the donors. In recent years, with more of an emphasis being placed on major gifts, this statistic has become 90/10 and is actually closing in on 95/5. Most organizations, however, spend 90 percent of their time dealing with approaches that reach the 90 percent of their donors who only give 10 percent of the contributions (direct mail, special events, etc). To be effective, 90 percent of the development office's time should be spent on identifying, cultivating, and soliciting the top 10 percent of its donors. A good software system can help the development office identify its current top 10 percent, and this group that can be put into a special category of major donors. A moves management system can then be developed to track movement among these top 10 percent.

In their article, *The Realities of Fund-Raising Costs and Accountability*, Stephen Smallwood and Wilson C. Levins supply illustrations that can help the organization to calculate percentage of expense to revenue, another helpful way to track costs of fundraising. Once the organization has these figures, it can compare its result to the acceptable standards listed by Greenfield.

ABC Institution Chart

Fundraising Cost Effectiveness Analysis for the Year Ending December 31, 20XX

	Revenue	Expenses	Net	Percentage of Expense to Revenue
New donor acquisition	116,000	135,000	(19,000)	116.4
Donor renewal	3,650,000	359,000	3,291,000	10.0

continued on the next page

	Revenue	Expenses	Net	Percentage of Expense to Revenue
Special events	104,000	18,000	86,000	17.3
Capital programs	692,000	78,000	614,000	11.3
Deferred gifts and bequests	481,000	56,000	425,000	11.6
Indirect campaigns	275,000	8,000	267,000	2.9
Total	5,318,000	654,000	4,664,000	12.3%

Return on Investment

The National Center for Charitable Statistics cites an example of how to calculate return on investment, which is often helpful for the development office to explain its costs to board members and other businesspeople, who are accustomed to thinking in these terms, and who can provide input for the development officer, who must decide if an effort is worth the costs. Their report states that "bottom line cost percentages alone are not a useful measure for internal management purposes and the performance of one kind of fundraising program cannot necessarily be evaluated against another."

ROI Analysis Annual/Periodic Fundraising Return on Investment
by Category of Fundraising Activity Illustration

					ROI Analysis		
Category of Fundraising Activity	Fund-raising Investments	Number of Gifts	Amount of Gifts	Average Size of Gift	ROI	Minimum ROI	Variance Above/ (Below)
	A	B	C	C/B	D5C/A	F	D−F
Capacity Building							
1. Non–income–producing capacity building	120,000	N/A	N/A	N/A	N/A	N/A	N/A

Category of Fund raising Activity	Fund raising Investments	Number of Gifts	Amount of Gifts	Average Size of Gift	ROI Analysis		
					ROI	Minimum ROI	Variance Above/ (Below)
2. Donor acquisition	380,000	13,400	275,000	20.52	72.40%	70%	4%
3. Special events/PR	43,300	450	24,000	53.33	55.8%	130.0%	−74.2%
Total capacity building	543,000	13,850	299,000	21.59	55.1%	N/A	N/A
Fundraising costs %	181.6%						
Net Income-Producing							
4. Donor renewal, soliciting prior donors under $1,000	162,000	28,000	940,000	33.57	580.2%	300%	280.2%
5. Special events fundraising	123,000	600	320,000	533	260.2%	200%	60.2%
6. Major individual gifts (soliciting prior donors $1,000 and up)	320,000	2,230	1,870,000	839	584.4%	400%	184.4%
7. Planned giving/estate planning (after 4–7 years of losses)	165,000	13	650,000	50,000	393.9%	500%	−106.1%
8. Capital and endowment campaigns	195,000	125	1,780,000	14,240	912.8%	650%	262.8%

continued on the next page

					ROI Analysis		
Category of Fund raising Activity	Fund Raising Investments	Number of Gifts	Amount of Gifts	Average Size of Gift	ROI	Minimum ROI	ROI Variance Above/ (Below)
9. Corporate and foundation grant seeking	85,000	16	480,000	30,000	564.7%	650%	−285.3%
10. Government grant seeking	15,000	2	100,000	50,000	666.7%	650%	16.7%
Total net income-producing	1,065,000	30,986	6,140,000	198	575.5%	N/A	N/A
Fundraising cost %	17.3%						
Grand total	1,6–8,000	44,836	6,439,000	144	400.4%	N/A	N/A
Fundraising cost %	25%						

While these calculations seem complex, the report states that "the time has come for the nonprofit sector to take a more sophisticated and business-like approach to these aspects of fundraising management." Being able to show return on investment is certainly a more positive approach than focusing solely on fundraising costs.

Other Benchmarking Standards

As outlined in the previous chapter, other standards to be measured in addition to the budget are the timelines for accomplishing tasks and the responsibilities of various individuals and work groups. The sample benchmarking lists (Exhibits 6.1–6.3) at the end of Chapter 6 show how to monitor the timeline and the areas of responsibility by comparing results to the stated deadlines and areas of responsibility in the plan.

TIPS & TECHNIQUES

When benchmarking results of the development plan, several steps will be helpful:

- Determine what accepted standards are most important for the organization to consider.

- Compare current results to accepted standards.

- Set realistic goals to improve those areas where the organization's results are not acceptable or need improvement.

- Establish timelines and budgets for each of these areas and assign someone to monitor results.

- Measure results on a quarterly basis and adjust strategies if necessary.

- Show the improvement in charts and graphs to the CEO and board, stressing the importance of investment in the development office for continuous improvement.

What If the Plan Is Not on Track?

Small adjustments are to be expected in any development plan, but what happens when the plan is seriously off track? This may be the result of setting unrealistic goals and objectives. When this is the case, the planning team should get together and revisit their original goals and objectives to determine what factors prevented these goals and objectives from being reached. Were there extenuating circumstances that were episodic and not believed to have a long-term effect on the development plan? If so, perhaps just adjusting the timelines will be required. However, if the organization has serious problems that are preventing goals and objectives from being implemented, then perhaps the plan should be revisited in light of these circumstances and more reasonable goals and objectives developed.

Monitoring the plan on a regular basis can prevent many of these circumstances from delaying the entire plan because adjustments can be made before the plan is seriously off track. It is much easier to get back on track if the plan is monitored on a regular basis. Going back to our example of the family moving from New York to San Francisco, if they get off on a wrong exit somewhere in Wyoming and stay on that course for hours and hours, they may find themselves hopelessly lost. However, if the navigator realizes soon after they've taken the wrong turn that they are headed in the opposite direction from where they should be, they can make a quick turn and get back on the main highway without losing a whole day of driving.

It is important that, in addition to the chief development officer (CDO), who has the primary responsibility for carrying out the plan, each individual and/or work group is held accountable for their aspect of the plan. Board members must be held accountable to make calls and hold cultivation events if that is part of the plan. The major gift efforts of the development office can be seriously delayed if the board and executive management are not doing their part to implement the plan.

Likewise, support staff must be aware of the overall plan and how important their particular aspects of the plan are in order to keep things on track. Every person, from the CDO to the receptionist in the development office, has an important role to play in keeping the plan on track, and regular staff meetings to review the plan can show each staff person that his or her function is critical to the plan's being successful. If one person falls down in his or her function, it will affect the entire plan. For example, gifts received in the mail during a phonathon not being entered into the system immediately could affect the volunteers who are asking people for pledges who may have already given, frustrating both the volunteers and the donors. This could have a drastic affect on the annual fund. This is just one small example of how the plan must function from a global perspective.

Summary

Benchmarking is critical to the success of the plan. Results should be measured against acceptable standards, and realistic goals and objectives should be put in place for improving on areas where results are not in accordance with accepted standards of practice.

The organization should also look at return on investment and understand that it is necessary to invest in the development office in order to improve results.

Organizations should focus their efforts on the 10 percent of their donors who are responsible for 90 percent of the gifts received. The development plan must include strategies to develop a moves management plan that focuses on ways to identify, cultivate, and solicit gifts from the top 10 percent of their donors.

Benchmarking steps include:

- Determining acceptable standards.

- Measuring current results against these standards.

- Establishing goals and objectives to improve these results and appointing someone to monitor results.

- Reporting results to CEO and board, stressing investment in continuous improvement.

When the development plan is seriously off track, the goals and objectives should be revisited to see if they were realistic.

Each person on the development team must be held accountable for his or her portion of the plan if the entire plan is to be successful.

Further Readings

Greenfield, James M. *Fund Raising,* 2nd ed. (New York: John Wiley & Sons, 1999).

The Urban Institute at Indiana University, *Donating to Charity: A Guide,* 2004.

Smallwood, Stephen J., and Wilson C. Levins, "The Realities of Fund-Raising Costs and Accountability," *Philanthropy Monthly,* September 1977.

National Center for Nonprofit Statistics and The Center on Philanthropy at Indiana University, *Nonprofit and Administrative Costs.*

Philanthropic Monthly, March 1993, pp. 23–37.

CHAPTER 8

The Next Step

*"The man (or woman) who views the world at fifty the same as
he (or she) did at twenty has wasted thirty years of his (or her) life."*
Muhammad Ali

After reading this chapter, you will be able to:

- Develop a plan to use the successes and failures of the plan in order to develop the next plan.
- Develop a timeline for the next development plan.

How Did It Work?

Looking back on the successes and failures of the plan and using the information to improve on the next plan is the final step in a successful planning process. In almost every instance, some of the goals will have been met or even exceeded, while others will fall short of expectations. The thing to remember is that the process of evaluating the plan in its final stages should help build on the strengths and overcome the weaknesses in this plan to improve the next plan.

Successes

It is important to celebrate success. Staff people who have been successful in exceeding financial goals, completing tasks ahead of schedule, increasing volunteer involvement, and the like should be recognized at staff meetings. The organization can prepare a chart listing goals and fill in goals as they are accomplished, give token gifts to those who have achieved outstanding successes, or publish successes in an internal newsletter.

Board members and other volunteers, in particular, should be made aware of their part in an objective's being reached successfully. The chief development officer (CDO) should always present a report on the plan's progress at board meetings and be present to answer questions the board might have. This is an excellent time to congratulate board members on their role in achieving success. Often, board members can be very competitive within the group when it comes to fundraising. Knowing the personality of the board will help the CDO decide how to best celebrate successes with this group. Some techniques might not work with a less aggressive group and some organizations frown on competitive activities, particularly faith-based groups and others that might have board members who are reluctant to receive public recognition. There is also a lot to be said for board members who fulfill their tasks because they really care about the organization and feel it is part of their job, not because of the public recognition that it entails. It is important to know and understand the motivations of the organization's board members.

Volunteer Fundraisers

For the organization that is using volunteers in its fundraising efforts, it is equally important to keep them apprised on progress regarding the development plan. The development committee, in particular, should be evaluating progress on a regular basis. For organizations that do not have a development office, this committee may be the primary evaluator of success. In either case, there should be time set aside at each development committee meeting to review progress on the plan. The chair of the development committee should lead the discussion with input from staff. The development committee chair should also report success to the board, again with the support of the development staff. This committee can

TIPS & TECHNIQUES

Recognizing Staff for Success

It is vital to celebrate the successful completion of segments of the plan. Some ideas for recognizing staff members who have done an outstanding job with their segment of the plan's implementation include:

- Having a special catered lunch brought in for the staff or taking them out for lunch.

- Posting a chart in the staff meeting room showing successful completion of tasks—be creative and use a chart that ties in with the organization's mission: a stack of books for a library, a child's growth chart for a youth-serving organization, a circle of people for a human service organization, and so on.

- A day off or half day off, especially around holidays or their birthday.

- A special lapel pin or other token gift that can be prominently displayed.

- A special parking place recognizing the development employee of the month.

- Recognition at an organization-wide event so the rest of the departments in the organization understand how important the development function is to the organization.

- Inviting staff to a board meeting where they can be recognized by the chair of the board or to a development committee meeting where the development committee chair recognizes their efforts.

- Lunch with the chief executive officer (CEO), who will recognize their efforts with a certificate or token gift.

IN THE REAL WORLD

Board Recognition

One organization posts a large billboard-type chart in its boardroom listing each board member by name. The chart then shows how each board member is doing in fundraising (see Exhibit 8.1 at the end of this chapter). Each board member is also given a printout of the results to add to his or her board manual. The executive director takes it one step further and carefully seats each board member in a strategic location; those who are not doing so well will be facing the wall with the chart so they can see how they stack up against other board members. As board members file into the room before the meeting starts, it is interesting to watch these board members comparing themselves and commenting on those who are doing well and those who are not.

congratulate the board on its success, which often encourages other board members to get involved in fundraising.

A note here on the makeup of the development committee is worthy of attention. The development committee should be chaired by a board member who will report progress of the committee to the board, including updates on the development plan. However, the development committee should also include non–board members, those who are not ready for the fiduciary responsibility of a board member but want to be involved in the organization's fundraising activities, or those who are brought onto the committee for their particular expertise, such as planned giving. This enables the organization to expand its network of potential funders as well as gain valuable expertise from members of the committee and groom potential board members. Because many of the development committee members may not be board members, it is important to recognize them as a separate committee at their committee meetings and at the board meetings.

One university holds a major corporate appeal each year, utilizing about 200 community business leaders as volunteers, working in teams of four to seven people. At the end of the campaign, a victory luncheon is held and prizes are given to the team that has raised the most money, the team that received the largest number of pledges, the individual team member who raised the most money, the individual team member who received the most pledges, the individual who brought in the first pledge, and so on. Prizes are generally things like restaurant gift certificates and other gifts-in-kind that the development office was able to secure. Competition is keen among teams from competing banks and other businesses, and although the prizes do not have a high dollar value, they are sought after because of the prestige of winning.

Other fundraising volunteers also should be involved in celebrating successes and being recognized for their part in the fundraising effort. This may include volunteers who work on the corporate appeal, phonathon volunteers, a planned giving council, and any other volunteers who are involved in the organization's fundraising activities. This can be done at a formal volunteer recognition event, through personal notes and phone calls, and by listing the volunteers' names in a newsletter, on the Web site, or in a newspaper ad. Most volunteers are happy to receive this public recognition.

Failures in the Plan

While celebrating successes publicly is important, it is equally critical not to chide staff members for not meeting objectives, especially in front of their coworkers. It is necessary, however, to make sure that staff members are accountable for implementing their part of the plan. If a particular staff member is having problems with his or her part of the plan, there may be other issues

One vice president of development required that all staff members report on a weekly basis, first thing Monday morning, on the progress made in each segment of the plan that fell within their responsibility. If staff members were not meeting timelines, budgets, or goals, they were asked to explain why. Often, there were extenuating circumstances that clearly explained what might be perceived as "failures" without a careful look at the circumstances causing this goal not to be met. For example, perhaps a direct mail piece did not get out on time because a major government grant deadline came up and this grant proposal could not be delayed. This method of evaluation helped the vice president tremendously because she could see if she was overly aggressive with some of her goals and deadlines. At the same time, it helped the staff people not to dwell on goals and objectives that were behind schedule, but to realistically budget their time by prioritizing tasks.

regarding this person's work that need to be addressed. Perhaps he or she is not the right person for this job, but could possibly be a valuable member of the development team in another position. Or perhaps there is an issue with the goals or objectives of that part of the plan. Or the individual charged with this section of the plan may not have the tools to perform the task. For example, if mailings are not getting out on time, the CDO must ask whether the database system is capable of handling bulk mail, or if more volunteers are needed to stuff mailings. The CDO needs to handle each case individually and work with staff to address problems that may be preventing them from fulfilling their part of the plan.

Board Members

Board members should also be held accountable for their role in implementing the plan. This insistence on accountability should come from the board chair and/or chair of the development committee. Once board members have bought into the goals and objectives and agreed to assume a role in implementing the development plan, they should be evaluated on an ongoing basis. It is also good to provide the board members with an annual evaluation of their performance overall as board members, and this evaluation should include an assessment of their fundraising performance. Some board assessment tools (Exhibits 8.1–8.3) may be found at the end of this chapter.

Other Volunteers

It is generally harder to hold a volunteer accountable for their performance than it is to require accountability for staff or even board members. For this reason, volunteers should be carefully identified, recruited, and trained. This can help ensure that they won't lose interest in the task. If the organization is faced with volunteers who do not deliver what they have previously agreed to, the plan will suffer from this lack of commitment. It is important that the CDO or the staff member who is working with these volunteers keep them on track. Phone calls and e-mails as gentle reminders are helpful. It is better to have a peer volunteer call them to remind them of their commitment to the organization, so a trusted, experienced volunteer in the leadership role is critical. The staff, however, should monitor and work with the volunteer chair to keep other volunteers on track.

IN THE REAL WORLD

One organization has its staff campaign coordinator send weekly e-mail reminders to each volunteer on the capital campaign committee, reporting successful asks and reminding people of the deadlines for their division to complete their calls. The chair of each division also receives copies of these e-mails, and follows up with a phone call to congratulate volunteers who have completed their calls and urge on those who are falling behind in their calls.

The Next Plan

When is it time to start planning for the next plan? Most development plans will have both short- and long-term goals. The short-term goals should be done on an annual basis. Once a full-blown plan is in place, and has been monitored and evaluated, it should be fairly easy to update the annual work plan based on the successes and failures of the previous plan.

Long-term goals, usually three to five years, should also be reviewed on an annual basis, if not more frequently, and updated as necessary. Often, when an organization is planning some major fundraising activity, such as a capital campaign, three to five years seems like a long time down the road, but deadlines tend to approach more rapidly than anticipated. If the long-term plans change, the short-range plan may be affected, for example, if the capital campaign gets pushed up a year earlier than originally anticipated because a prime piece of real estate becomes available at a great price, a landlord offers the organization a deep discount for getting out of a lease early, and the like. In cases like this, the organization may need to shift gears rather dramatically. The capital campaign may now take precedence over some other new activities that the organization was considering, or the annual campaign may now become part of a comprehensive campaign. *Flexibility* must be the middle name of all development officers.

As one plan year ends, the development office should be gearing up to do the next plan during the last month of the existing plan.

Keeping the plan on track, while allowing for changes in circumstances, is one of the most challenging aspects of the development plan, but one that must be handled by the CDO if the plan is to have any meaning. With proper planning, flexibility, and perseverance, the development plan will be one of the best tools to help the development program grow.

Summary

Evaluating the plan on a regular basis and being able to handle successes and failures is the key to making a development plan work.

Success should be celebrated publicly. Rewarding and recognizing staff, board members, and other fundraising volunteers is critical to keeping them enthused about the plan.

Recognizing failures in the plan is equally important, but failures on the part of any individual or group should be handled individually with that person or group. Sometimes it is necessary to reevaluate and adjust the plan because of these failures. Other times, it may require working closely with the group or individual in charge of that aspect of the plan to determine why it is not working and deal with the issues at hand.

All who are involved in the plan—staff, board, and volunteers—must be held accountable for their portion of the plan.

The plan must also be flexible enough to adapt to major changes within the organization or the environment.

As one plan's timeline is coming to an end, the organization must learn how to build on the successes and overcome the failures in this plan in order to develop the next plan.

The development plan requires that the development office and the organization remain flexible, but persevere in the goals. Those who have learned this lesson will be able to plan their work and work their plan.

EXHIBIT 8.1

XYZ Organization Board of Directors
Fundraising Progress

Board Member	Annual Gift	Golf Tournament Sponsors	Golf Tournament Teams	Gala Tables Sold	Gala Sponsors	Gifts in Kind	Major Gifts
Adams, Alice							
Baker, Ann							
Collins, Tom							
Dean, Donald							
Edison, Tom							
Frank, Francis							
George, Bob							
Harris, Linda							
Johnson, Joe							
Kline, Carol							
Lewis, Bob							
Martin, Max							

Nelson, Pam					
Parker, Peter					
Ruiz, Magdalena					
Silverberg, Sam					
Thomas, Tim					
Ulrich, Sandy					
Washington, Lou					

Board Member Name	Offices or Committee Chairs Held	Committee Served On	Board Member's Term Expires	Member's Average Annual Gift	Active fund raiser? Yes/No	How much time has this board member given for the org. High/Med/Low

EXHIBIT 8.3

Board Fundraising Assessment Form

1. What percentage of the board makes a meaningful financial commitment to the organization on an annual basis?

    _____ 100% (10)   _____ 40% (4)

    _____ 90% (9)   _____ 30% (3)

    _____ 80% (8)   _____ 20% (2)

    _____ 70% (7)   _____ 10% (1)

    _____ 60% (6)   _____ 0% (0)

    _____ 50% (5)   POINTS _____

2. What percentage of the board has made a planned gift to the organization?

    _____ 100% (10)   _____ 40% (4)

    _____ 90% (9)   _____ 30% (3)

    _____ 80% (8)   _____ 20% (2)

    _____ 70% (7)   _____ 10% (1)

    _____ 60% (6)   _____ 0% (0)

    _____ 50% (5)   POINTS _____

3. What percentage of the board made a contribution to the last capital campaign run by the organization (where applicable)?

    _____ 100% (10)   _____ 40% (4)

    _____ 90% (9)   _____ 30% (3)

    _____ 80% (8)   _____ 20% (2)

    _____ 70% (7)   _____ 10% (1)

    _____ 60% (6)   _____ 0% (0)

    _____ 50% (5)   POINTS _____

continued on the next page

4. What percentage of the board attends events held by the organization?

    _____ 100% (10)   _____ 40% (4)

    _____ 90% (9)   _____ 30% (3)

    _____ 80% (8)   _____ 20% (2)

    _____ 70% (7)   _____ 10% (1)

    _____ 60% (6)   _____ 0% (0)

    _____ 50% (5)   POINTS _____

5. The board helps develop our long-range and annual development (fundraising) plan?

    _____ Yes, all are involved (10)

    _____ Some are involved (5)

    _____ None are involved (0)   POINTS _____

6. The board is involved in recruiting volunteer fundraisers?

    _____ Yes, all are involved (10)

    _____ Some are involved (5)

    _____ None are involved (0)   POINTS _____

7. The board helps identify potential donors to the organization?

    _____ Yes, all are involved (10)

    _____ Some are involved (5)

    _____ None are involved (0)   POINTS _____

8. The board plans and attends cultivation events regularly?

    _____ Yes, all are involved (10)

    _____ Some are involved (5)

    _____ None are involved (0)   POINTS _____

9. The board has an adequate number of people with affluence and influence in the community?

___ All (10)

___ Some (5)

___ None (0)   POINTS ___

10. The board understands that each member has a sphere of influence that can be helpful to the organization, and members are willing to promote the organization within their own sphere of influence?

___ Yes, all are involved (10)

___ Some are involved (5)

___ None are involved (0)   POINTS ___

TOTAL POINTS ___

A score of 75 or higher means your board is sufficiently involved in fundraising activities; 50-74, your board needs some work; and under 50 means your board needs a great deal of work.

A Donor Bill of Rights

PHILANTHROPY is based on voluntary action for the common good. It is a tradition of giving and sharing that is primary to the quality of life. To assure that philanthropy merits the respect and trust of the general public, and that donors and prospective donors can have full confidence in the not-for-profit organizations and causes they are asked to support, we declare that all donors have these rights:

I.

To be informed of the organization's mission, of the way the organization intends to use donated resources, and of its capacity to use donations effectively for their intended purposes.

II.

To be informed of the identity of those serving on the organization's governing board, and to expect the board to exercise prudent judgement in its stewardship responsibilities.

III.

To have access to the organization's most recent financial statements.

IV.

To be assured their gifts will be used for the purposes for which they were given.

V.

To receive appropriate acknowledgement and recognition.

VI.

To be assured that information about their donations is handled with respect and with confidentiality to the extent provided by law.

VII.

To expect that all relationships with individuals representing organizations of interest to the donor will be professional in nature.

VIII.

To be informed whether those seeking donations are volunteers, employees of the organization, or hired solicitors.

IX.

To have the opportunity for their names to be deleted from mailing lists that an organization may intend to share.

X.

To feel free to ask questions when making a donation and to receive prompt, truthful and forthright answers.

DEVELOPED BY

Association for Healthcare Philanthropy (AHP)
Association of Fundraising Professionals (AFP)
Council for Advancement and Support of Education (CASE)
Giving Institute: Leading Consultants to Non-Profits

ENDORSED BY

(in formation)
Independent Sector
National Catholic Development Conference (NCDC)
National Committee on Planned Giving (NCPG)
Council for Resource Development (CRD)
United Way of America

AFP Code of Ethical Principles and Standards of Professional Practice

STATEMENT OF ETHICAL PRINCIPLES

Adopted 1964, Amended October 2004

Association of
Fundraising Professionals

The Association of Fundraising Professionals (AFP) exists to foster the development and growth of fundraising professionals and the profession, to promote high ethical standards in the fundraising profession and to preserve and enhance philanthropy and volunteerism. Members of AFP are motivated by an inner drive to improve the quality of life through the causes they serve. They serve the ideal of philanthropy; are committed to the preservation and enhancement of volunteerism; and hold stewardship of these concepts as the overriding principle of their professional life. They recognize their responsibility to ensure that needed resources are vigorously and ethically sought and that the intent of the donor is honestly fulfilled. To these ends, AFP members embrace certain values that they strive to uphold in performing their responsibilities for generating philanthropic support.

AFP members aspire to:

+ practice their profession with integrity, honesty, truthfulness and adherence to the absolute obligation to safeguard the public trust;
+ act according to the highest standards and visions of their organization, profession and conscience;
+ put philanthropic mission above personal gain;
+ inspire others through their own sense of dedication and high purpose;
+ improve their professional knowledge and skills so that their performance will better serve others;
+ demonstrate concern for the interests and well being of individuals affected by their actions;
+ value the privacy, freedom of choice and interests of all those affected by their actions;
+ foster cultural diversity and pluralistic values, and treat all people with dignity and respect;
+ affirm, through personal giving, a commitment to philanthropy and its role in society;
+ adhere to the spirit as well as the letter of all applicable laws and regulations;
+ advocate within their organizations, adherence to all applicable laws and regulations;
+ avoid even the appearance of any criminal offense or professional misconduct;
+ bring credit to the fundraising profession by their public demeanor;
+ encourage colleagues to embrace and practice these ethical principles and standards of professional practice; and
+ be aware of the codes of ethics promulgated by other professional organizations that serve philanthropy.

STANDARDS OF PROFESSIONAL PRACTICE

Furthermore, while striving to act according to the above values, AFP members agree to abide by the *AFP Standards of Professional Practice*, which are adopted and incorporated into the *AFP Code of Ethical Principles*. Violation of the *Standard* may subject the member to disciplinary sanctions, including expulsion, as provided in the AFP Ethics Enforcement Procedures.

Professional Obligations

1. Members shall not engage in activities that harm the member's organization, clients, or profession.
2. Members shall not engage in activities that conflict with their fiduciary, ethical and legal obligations to their organizations and their clients.
3. Members shall effectively disclose all potential and actual conflicts of interest; such disclosure does not preclude or imply ethical impropriety.
4. Members shall not exploit any relationship with a donor, prospect, volunteer or employee for the benefit of the member or the member's organization.

5. Members shall comply with all applicable local, state, provincial, federal, civil and criminal laws.
6. Members recognize their individual boundaries of competence and are forthcoming and truthful about their professional experience and qualifications.

Solicitation and Use of Philanthropic Funds

7. Members shall take care to ensure that all solicitation materials are accurate and correctly reflect the organization's mission and use of solicited funds.
8. Members shall take care to ensure that donors receive informed, accurate and ethical advice about the value and tax implications of contributions.
9. Members shall take care to ensure that contributions are used in accordance with donors' intentions.
10. Members shall take care to ensure proper stewardship of philanthropic contributions, including timely reports on the use and management of such funds.
11. Members shall obtain explicit consent by the donor before altering the conditions of contributions.

Presentation of Information

12. Members shall not disclose privileged or confidential information to unauthorized parties.
13. Members shall adhere to the principle that all donor and prospect information created by, or on behalf of, an organization is the property of that organization and shall not be transferred or utilized except on behalf of that organization.
14. Members shall give donors the opportunity to have their names removed from lists that are sold to, rented to, or exchanged with other organizations.
15. Members shall, when stating fundraising results, use accurate and consistent accounting methods that conform to the appropriate guidelines adopted by the American Institute of Certified Public Accountants (AICPA)* for the type of organization involved. (* In countries outside of the United States, comparable authority should be utilized.)

Compensation

16. Members shall not accept compensation that is based on a percentage of contributions; nor shall they accept finder's fees.
17. Members may accept performance-based compensation, such as bonuses, provided such bonuses are in accord with prevailing practices within the members' own organizations, and are not based on a percentage of contributions.
18. Members shall not pay finder's fees, or commissions or percentage compensation based on contributions, and shall take care to discourage their organizations from making such payments.

Amended October 2004

AFP / Wiley Fund Development Series

Beyond Fund Raising: New Strategies for Nonprofit Innovation and Investment, Second Edition
Kay Sprinkel Grace, CFRE
ISBN 0-471-70713-9

This new edition looks particularly at the stewardship tools available through the Internet, the impact of accountability on planning, streamlined ideas regarding capital campaigns and feasibility studies, new techniques for annual giving that recognize the impact of the Internet, and new ways to involve increasingly busy board members in organizations. Retaining its primary focus on values and mission-based philanthropy, and on other key tenets of Kay Sprinkel Grace's beliefs and practices, this new edition will take readers through the next decade just as the first edition has guided them through the last.

Capital Campaigns from the Ground Up: How Nonprofits Can Have the Building of Their Dreams
Stanley Weinstein, ACFRE
ISBN 0-471-22079-5

This book provides decision makers with essential tools for realizing their organization's highest possible development hopes. Written by veteran nonprofit planner and campaigner Stanley Weinstein, this book is unique in discussing fundraising preparation together with building planning. The resulting overview clearly lays out a balanced, thoughtful program for successful project development.

Careers in Fundraising
Lilya Wagner, EdD, CFRE
ISBN 0-471-40359-8

Careers in Fundraising provides expert guidance on professional opportunities in the field of fundraising, including topics on professional development, on-the-job issues, and the significance of fundraising as a career. This comprehensive resource covers all aspects of the profession, and also addresses the personal mission and commitment necessary for success in the field.

The Complete Guide to Fundraising Management, Second Edition
Stanley Weinstein, ACFRE
ISBN 0-471-20019-0

This book is a practical management how-to, tailored specifically to the needs of fundraisers. Moving beyond theory, it addresses the day-to-day problems faced in these organizations and offers hands-on advice and practical solutions. The book and accompanying include sample CD-ROM customizable forms, checklists, and grids that will help the reader plan and execute complicated fundraising campaigns.

Critical Issues in Fund Raising
Dwight F. Burlingame, PhD, CFRE, editor
ISBN 0-471-17465-3

Examines the most pressing issues facing fundraising professionals today. Extensive chapters cover donors, innovative fundraising, marketing, financial management, ethics, international philanthropy, and the fundraising professional. Written by a team of highly respected practitioners and educators, this book was developed in conjunction with AFP, the Council for the Advancement and Support of Education, the Association for Research on Nonprofit Organizations and Voluntary Action, and the Indiana University Center on Philanthropy.

Cultivating Diversity in Fundraising
Janice Gow Pettey, CFRE
ISBN 0-471-40361-X

Cultivating Diversity in Fundraising offers an overview in cultivating successful fundraising and an enhanced understanding of philanthropic motivation in four selected racial/ethnic populations—African American, Asian American (Chinese, Filipino, Japanese, Korean, and South Asian), Hispanic/Latino (Cuban, Dominican, El Salvadoran, Mexican, and Puerto Rican), and Native American. By understanding the rich philanthropic traditions of the individuals they are working with and soliciting funds from, fundraisers will be better equipped to serve their communities and their organizations.

Direct Response Fund Raising: Mastering New Trends for Results
Michael Johnston
ISBN 0-471-38024-5

This guide offers fundraisers, managers, and volunteers an excellent understanding of how to plan and execute successful direct response campaigns. The success of a nonprofit direct response program requires staying on top of recent trends in the field. These trends include appealing more effectively to aging baby boomers as well as tapping into powerful new databases, the Internet, CD-ROMs, diskettes, and videos. The book includes a CD-ROM, with all the full-color, complete examples from the book as well as many more.

Ethical Decision-Making in Fund Raising
Marilyn Fischer, PhD
ISBN 0-471-28943-3

A handbook for ethical reasoning and discussion. In her provocative new book, Dr. Fischer provides conceptual tools with which a nonprofit can thoroughly examine the ethics of how and from whom it seeks donations. With the book's Ethical Decision–Making Model, the author explains how fundraisers can use their basic value commitments to organizational mission, relationships, and integrity as day-to-day touchstones for making balanced, ethical fundraising decisions.

The Fund Raiser's Guide to the Internet
Michael Johnston
ISBN 0-471-25365-0

This book presents the issues, technology, and resources involved in online fundraising and donor relations. A practical "how-to" guide, it presents real-world case studies and successful practices from a top consulting firm, as well as guidance, inspiration, and warnings to nonprofits learning to develop this new fundraising technique. It also covers such important factors as determining your market, online solicitation pieces, security issues, and setting up your Web site.

Fundraising Fundamentals: A Guide to Annual Giving for Professionals and Volunteers, Second Edition
James M. Greenfield, ACFRE, FAHP
ISBN 0-471-20987-2

A comprehensive step-by-step guide to the fundamentals of fundraising, with practical how-to advice on the basic methods and techniques necessary to carry out successful annual giving campaigns. Subjects covered include: direct mail solicitation, telemarketing, renewals, membership drives, special events, volunteer fundraising, and more.

The Legislative Labyrinth: A Map for Not-for-Profits
Walter P. Pidgeon, Jr., PhD, CFRE
ISBN 0-471-40069-6

Currently, only a fraction of the nonprofit community takes advantage of the legislative process in representing their members and furthering its missions. Nonprofits are missing a significant way to fulfill their mission of gaining visibility and attracting new members and funding sources. This book answers the questions of nonprofits thinking of starting a lobbying program.

The Nonprofit Handbook: Fund Raising, Third Edition
James M. Greenfield, ACFRE, FAHP
ISBN 0-471-40304-0

The third edition of this invaluable handbook provides a complete overview of the entire development function, from management and strategic planning to hands-on, practical guidance for the various kinds of fundraising. Written by leading fundraising professionals, edited by James M. Greenfield, this essential resource brings together over 70 contributors who are vanguard experts and professionals in the field of fundraising.

Nonprofit Essentials: Endowment Building
Diana S. Newman
ISBN 0-471-67846-5

This is a complete overview of the critical process of securing a nonprofit's future. The book outlines the step-by-step process for developing and implementing an endowment program. In practical, down-to-earth terms, it covers making the case for endowments (involving the board and securing the support of members), raising funds (planned giving and special events), investing the money (asset allocation and spending policies), marketing (preparing a strategic marketing plan), and much more.

Nonprofit Essentials: The Capital Campaign
Julia Ingraham Walker
ISBN 0-471-68429-5

This book is a clear and compelling guide to the key components shared by all campaigns: campaign preparation, leadership prospect identification, making the case for support, providing effective campaign leadership, prospect cultivation and solicitation, and donor recognition and stewardship. Illuminating case studies, practical tools, proven strategies, and helpful hints displayed throughout the book highlight solutions to common stumbling blocks that can trip up even the experienced campaign professional.

Nonprofit Investment Policies: Practical Steps for Growing Charitable Funds
Robert P. Fry, Jr., Esq.
ISBN 0-471-17887-X

Written in plain English by an investment manager who specializes in non-profit organizations, *Nonprofit Investment Policies* explores the unique characteristics of nonprofit investing. Covered topics include endowment management, planned gift assets, socially responsible investing, and more. This book includes charts and graphs to illustrate complex investment concepts, tables and checklists to guide nonprofit managers in decision making, and case studies of organizations of various sizes to show how to successfully develop and implement investment policies.

Planned Giving Simplified: The Gift, the Giver, and the Gift Planner
Robert F. Sharpe, Sr.
ISBN 0-471-16674-X

This resource, written by a well-known veteran of planned giving, is a down-to-earth introduction to the complex world of planned giving, a sophisticated fundraising strategy that involves big money, complex tax laws, and delicate personal politics. This book shows charities, and in particular the charities' planned givers, how to understand the process—both the administration of planned gifts as well as the spirit of giving.

The Universal Benefits of Volunteering
Walter P. Pidgeon, Jr., PhD, CFRE
ISBN 0-471-18505-1

Volunteering is good for nonprofits, individuals, and corporations because it builds strong interpersonal and professional skills that carry over into all sectors. A concise, hands-on guide to maximizing the use of business professionals in the nonprofit volunteer context, this workbook is a vital resource for all those involved in volunteering efforts. Included is a disk with all the worksheets and model documents needed to establish effective, successful, and ongoing volunteer programs.

Index